Hallé Flutes

Flautists of The Hallé Orchestra

1858 - 93

STUART SCOTT

First Published 1998

by S.J. Scott
6, Colville Grove,
Sale, Cheshire M33 4FW.

Printed by Kall Kwik, Altrincham, Cheshire.

ISBN 0 9532512 0 9

Cover Photograph: E.S. Redfern

Song is the spirit of thy flute

Which, bursting forth in rippling trills

Lulls the senses into dreams -

Again, as full of life as mystic rose,

And then like Etna's fiery stream -

It wooes in melody the Realm of Beauty

And wakes and melts the heart to tears.

BERNARD TAYLOR

ACKNOWLEDGEMENTS

The writing of this book would have been impossible without the generous assistance of Hallé members past and present and much encouragement offered by Joan Simpkin and Tony Walker who also provided archive material and numerous contacts. Robert Sheldon at the Dayton C. Miller Collection, Library of Congress, Washington D.C, contributed much useful information and photographic material, and Chris Steward very kindly compiled the list of early broadcasts.

My thanks go the the Hallé Concerts Society, Boosey & Hawkes, Alice Barlow, Robert Bigio, Andrew Fairley, Jenny Gulland, Joan Miller, Jane Morse and Clifford Seville for providing photographs and other material; also to numerous other people to whom I spoke during my research.

S. S. 1997

FOREWORD

In 1958 I placed an order with Rudall Carte & Co. at 24 Berners Street, London for a thin-throughout cocus wood flute with silver keys and a Brossa F# key. This cost the princely sum of £191.17s.6d. Little did I realise then that one day I would have the opportunity to occupy the seat once held by Jean Brossa in the Hallé Orchestra.

The previous encumbants of this prestigious chair were all distinguished players of great character and musicianship. Fortunately I have had the pleasure of knowing four of them. Douglas Townshend and I were serving in the Brigade of Guards about the same time. Oliver Bannister was in the orchestra when I came to Manchester in 1961. Peter Lloyd and I spent six years together in the BBC Northern Orchestra and Geoffrey Gilbert was instrumental in arranging for me to teach at the Royal Manchester College of Music.

I have been with the orchestra now for 30 years and during that time I have made music with many loyal friends and colleagues. We have taken our tradition of playing not only throughout the United Kingdom but all over the world. The Hallé sound is unique for its warmth, colour and musicality and it has been a privilege to have taken part in the life of such a great orchestra.

Stuart is to be congratulated on the dedication he has given to this history of the flute players of the Hallé Orchestra and I wish the book well. Perhaps in 139 years there will be another volume to accompany this one!

ROGER ROSTRON
Heaton Moor
Stockport

30th April 1997

Contents

INTRODUCTION

Manchester has long been a centre of activity for flautists and we all know that the Hallé Orchestra and the BBC Orchestra have had a long line of distinguished players but it may be of interest to note that long before these orchestras came into being an organisation of no fewer than twenty six flautists established the Gentlemen's Concerts there in 1774. In the 1780's, the Gentlemen's Concerts orchestra flautists included Samuel Taylor (son of the concert room doorkeeper), Nicholson, father of the celebrated flautist (a frequent performer in the area), and Andrew Ashe (1759-1841) who was first flute with the opera orchestra in Brussels and later directed his own concerts in Bath before retiring to Dublin in 1822.

In writing of the Gentlemen's Concerts, J. Ashton, in his "A Picture of Manchester" tells us that " Flute players mustered so strongly at all gatherings that the managers were obliged to make a rule that the flute gentlemen should take it in turns to play". From 1777 until around 1865, the Gentlemen's Concerts orchestra was always half amateurs and half professional musicians but after 1865 members of the Hallé Orchestra provided the orchestral music at all their concerts with Edward de Jong as a frequent soloist.

Names and details of the musicians who founded the Gentlemen's Concerts are largely forgotten these days but their legacy to us remains in the form of numerous very active amateur and professional groups, all containing their fair share of flautist talent. For many years Manchester has had musical training establishments capable of fostering such talent and enthusiasm as is found in those names which have appeared in concert programmes over the last 130 years or so, and much of that talent has been before the public in connection with the world renowned Hallé Orchestra.

The orchestra was formed in the mid-nineteenth century during a period of great invention for the flute when almost all aspects of the instrument were being modified, changed or improved. Many metal flutes were made with extended upper and lower registers suitable for solo and orchestral work and many modifications and additions to the Boehm system flute were made. One such addition to the fingering system was made by Hallé principal, Jean Firmin Brossa (1839-1915) who invented an F# touch key which became more common than other similar devices and was usually included in Boehm flute mechanisms as an optional extra. It is still in use on many flutes today. Of the numerous models available in the nineteenth century professional flautists eventually took up the Boehm flute unanimously and most British orchestral musicians by the end of the century were using Rudall Carte Boehm system cocuswood flutes.

Some players of this period had undertaken several changes of instrument during their careers. One Hallé principal, E.S. Redfern (1866-1921) had started flute playing using an old system flute but quickly changed to a Boehm system cocuswood flute as other players of his time had done but at the turn of the century we find him singing the praises of a Conn Wonder metal flute.

By the time the twentieth century arrived flautists still had a wide choice of instruments but whereas before there were a large number of fingering systems available, now all the flute makers were providing a selection of materials and a few supplementary keys for the Boehm system flutes. Orchestral players were using instruments made of wood, silver, gold and nickel. In 1950 Geoffrey Gilbert (1914-1989) who had been a member of the Hallé Orchestra in his early career, purchased and performed on a platinum flute for a short time but at the same time other flautists, and those of the Hallé, were still using wooden instruments producing a tonal blend of dense, firmly centred sound characteristic of British orchestras in the first half of this century. British players were strong supporters of the wooden flute and the majority were still playing on Rudall Carte cocuswood instruments well into the twentieth century. The present Hallé principal, Roger Rostron, retained a wooden instrument until the 1980's.

The mechanical changes of the nineteenth century were difficult enough to cope with for solo performers but at the same time these changes were assisting them in their quest for virtuosic effects. This striving after effect was seen by some as actively discouraging good quality compositions for the flute and there was at that time a lack of flute music by reputable composers. Among the early Hallé players, Edward de Jong (1837-1920) and Fred Lax (1858-1925) regretted this situation and tried their hand at composition presenting their efforts to the public in Britain and abroad helping to bring the flute back into favour with musicians, audiences and composers.

Training and experience in the late nineteenth and early twentieth century differed greatly from that of more recent times. Then, flautists gained experience in a variety of ensembles. The Carl Rosa Opera Company and others flourished in the 1890's and regularly gave performances in Manchester. There were also theatres, cinemas and seaside orchestras and players became extremely good sight readers over a short period of time. Not only that but they were flexible players with great awareness of ensemble and always technically assured. They were proud of their achievements and principals often showed their prowess in solo pieces accompanied by the rest of the orchestra.

Until the 1940's members of the Hallé Orchestra were also members of the Liverpool Philharmonic and BBC Northern Orchestra. In addition to this many played in other ensembles, festivals and seasonal orchestras so they were kept fairly busy. They were in effect, freelance players who got paid only for the engagements booked. Many of them had little formal training as we know it today but found that the advice of their teachers plus varied experiences served them adequately. Later, many players of the early Hallé years took on teaching appointments at the Royal Manchester College of Music or privately and so started a long line of teacher-pupil relationships in Hallé players spanning more than 100 years, establishing a tradition which is unique in British orchestras.

In more recent times training and experience have still been gained from renowned teachers who are also performers but longer formal training at the best musical institutions and scholarships to attend such institutions abroad is the order of the day. All these establishments run courses in orchestral work and nowadays there are excellent youth orchestras as well as freelance work available to students through music clubs and competitions through which young players gain experience. In the days of National Service players also found military bands good training grounds.

With the advent of more formal training and the possibilities for both teachers and pupils to travel abroad more freely came a widespread acceptance of the French style of playing and total eclipse of the traditional British School of playing. In the nineteenth century the use of wooden flutes produced a dense and in some respects more powerful sound than the silver flutes adopted later. This sound required more air pressure in blowing and a harder attack with the tongue as well as a tighter embouchure. Often the flute was pressed fairly hard against the lips and the resultant sound was very rich and almost reedy in character. The flautists did not use vibrato, preferring a straight steady tone instead. Even in the twentieth century the orchestral use of vibrato is strictly controlled so that woodwinds blend well. In the 1930's Geoffrey Gilbert adopted the French style of playing using a silver Louis Lot flute and through teaching and performing he influenced many others to follow him and even flautists using wooden flutes were persuaded to play with a more relaxed style. So the days of the traditional English flute sound were definitely at an end, and of course this eventually had an effect on the sound of British orchestras.

Orchestral flautists have held an honoured position amongst all instrumental players since the very beginnings of the modern symphony orchestra and they have great responsibilities of course. Not only is a flautist required to be a soloist but also to have the ability to blend sensitively as a chamber musician or to dominate huge orchestral climaxes. It is at such climaxes that the flute can be instantly isolated by the ear and this is because of the method used to produce the sound which is perhaps the purest and most natural of all woodwind instruments giving notes which are virtually free of overtones.

Lest we forget, the following pages contain details of flautists who have held honoured positions in the Hallé Orchestra and who by virtue of their musicianship and place in history have helped shape not only a great orchestra but subsequent generations of flute players who still enthrall us today.

Edward De Jong   © Andrew Fairley

HALLÉ'S FIRST FLUTE

The 1850's saw Manchester music being more organised and being brought into line with world trends. Charles Hallé and Louis Jullien were largely instrumental in this and with a concert in December 1856, Hallé held the interest of his audience with what was probably the first public performance in Manchester of Beethoven's 'Emperor' Concerto. About this time Louis Jullien (1812-1860) was putting on concerts with his own orchestra which were of a more popular character and he gained popularity for both himself and the music he presented through showmanship, flamboyance and musicianship. He spared no expense in engaging world famous soloists and orchestral musicians of the highest rank and accomplished more towards the spread of orchestral music among the Manchester populace than either Hallé or anyone else at that time. Jullien often presented his own skillfully composed quadrilles and being a piccolo soloist himself performed on numerous occasions to the delight of his audiences.

Edward de Jong (1837-1920) had been a member of Jullien's orchestra and working under Jullien had a lasting effect on him. The name of Edward de Jong had also been associated with Hallé's ventures and almost a year before Jullien's 'Farewell Concert' on New Years Day 1859, he had been appointed principal flute in Hallé's orchestra. De Jong had played in the Arts Treasures Exhibition Orchestra of 1857 which was an augmented orchestra of Hallé's Gentleman's Concerts, engaged especially for the Exhibition. Hallé was so pleased with the Exhibition performances that he decided to keep the band together and on October 22nd 1857 his new orchestra, with de Jong as principal flute of course, performed in the Free Trade Hall under his direction, but it wasn't until January 30th 1858 that the Hallé Orchestra as we know it today gave its first public orchestral concert in the Free Trade Hall, Manchester.

For its first season the orchestra had two flute players - De Jong as principal and a Mr Berry as second. Jullien's influence on De Jong's music making and on Hallé's concert organisation was now apparent as Hallé was giving his first real public concert series inviting the masses to his concerts by allocating a proportion of cheap seats, and De Jong was maintaining a high profile with regular solo performances beginning on September 29th 1858 with Boehm's Fantasia on Scottish Airs at the Wednesday concerts. In November of the same year he continued with a Grand Selection from Il Travatore on the 10th and Boehm's Fantasia on Beethoven's 'Le Desir' on the 17th. Indeed Boehm's works seemed to have figured highly in De Jong's repertoire at this time as there were performances of the Fantasia on German Airs (Jan 5th 1859), Fantasia on Swiss Airs (March 16th 1859) and the Fantasia on 'Swiss Boy' (April 18th 1860).

In November 1859 Hallé started his second season of public concerts and now Mr Berry (second flute) was replaced by R. Charlton who remained with the orchestra until De Jong left in 1870. Between November 1858 and January 1865 De Jong played thirteen solos including his own Scotch Airs, Fantasia on Faust and Fantasia on Lucia di Lammermoor. During this period he also featured solos by other well known flautists - Furstenau's Fantasia on Norma, Richardson's There's nae luck, Briccialdi's Fantasia on Airs from Lucrezia Borgia and Paggi's Fantasie on Neopolitan Airs. Fellow Dutchman Jules Demersseman was included too on January 12th 1865 when De Jong took part in a performance of the Grand Duet for flute and oboe with his friend and colleague Mons. Lavigne taking the oboe part. The duet was repeated on December 28th of the same year and the two players were to perform together again almost a year later on December 6th 1866 when on that occasion they gave S. Jacoby's Duet on Scotch Airs. The last time De Jong performed as soloist at a Hallé Concert was on January 31st 1867 when he played his own rather difficult Fantasia on Faust.

Three years followed with no opportunity for solo work when Hallé's concerts saw an increase in vocal solo appearances and piano solos given by Charles Hallé himself. This no doubt influenced De Jong's decision to leave the orchestra and set up his own Saturday Popular Concerts providing music for the populace more in the style of Jullien. Hallé considered this a rival venture and refused to allow his players to accept engagements with De Jong and in consequence he lost several good musicians at that time, one of which was Mons. Lavigne the oboist with whom De Jong had worked closely during his time as Hallé principal. De Jong had an orchestra of sixty players, the flautists being John Taylor (principal) and Eugene Damaré (piccolo). Damaré (1840 - 1919) had previously toured with the Arban Band and eventually wrote more than 400 pieces, numerous studies and a method in three volumes but is now only known for his solo 'The Wren". He was often featured as piccolo soloist at De Jong's concerts and after a performance on January 1st 1874 a Manchester critic wrote - "M. Damaré played some most brilliant and effective variations on the Carnival de Venice in a manner of which it would be almost impossible to speak too highly".

At the same concert De Jong played the flute obbligato to a performance of Ciardi's "L'usignuolo" given by Madame Sinico, Mons. Lavigne played his own Fantasia on Airs from 'Mirella' and for the evening performance Demersseman's Duet for flute and oboe replaced Lavigne's solo. The format and content of this concert and all the other Saturday Popular Concerts followed in the style of Jullien and indeed Jullien put in an appearance at the above mentioned New Years Day Concert in the form of a performance of his Quadrille, "British Army". Needless to say, De Jong had spared no expense in augmenting his forces for this concert having secured the services of four soloists, the 7th Dragoon Guards, The 95th Regiment, the Drum and Fife Bands of the 95th Regiment, the 56th Lancashire (Salford) Volunteers and the Pipers of the Scots Fusileer Guards!

FREE TRADE HALL, MANCHESTER.

MR. DE JONG'S
POPULAR CONCERTS.

TWO EXTRA PERFORMANCES ON NEW-YEAR'S DAY.

VOCALIST:

MADAME SINICO.

Solo Piccolo - - - - - Mons. DAMARÉ.

Solo Flute - - - - - Mr. DE JONG.

Solo Oboe - - - - - Mons. LAVIGNE.

By kind permission of their respective commanding officers, the MILITARY BANDS of the

7TH DRAGOON GUARDS, THE 95TH REGIMENT,

THE

DRUM AND FIFE BANDS

OF THE

95th Regiment and the 56th. Lancashire (Salford) Volunteers,

AND THE

PIPERS OF THE SCOTS FUSILIER GUARDS

WILL BE ADDED TO MR. DE JONG'S ORCHESTRA.

Morning Performance to commence at 2-30; Evening Performance at 7-30.

PRICES OF ADMISSION — GALLERY-STALLS *(reserved and cushioned)* 4s.; GALLERY, 2s.; AREA SEATS, 2s.; BODY, 1s.; BOXES, £1. 1s.

Children for Morning Performances only—Gallery Stalls, 2s.; Gallery, 1s.

Plan can be seen and tickets may be obtained at Hime and Addison's, 30, Victoria-street, and at Box Office, Free Trade Hall. Holders of Gallery and Body Tickets purchased prior to the doors being opened will be admitted at the usual entrance for morning performances at 1-30, and evening performances at 6-15. The doors will be opened to the general public—Morning performance at 2-0, and evening performance at 6-45.

Price 2d.

So for now De Jong's concerts continued to please both the public and the critics but the previous year (1873) he had put on Messiah, Midsummer Night's Dream and Judas Maccabeus which proved not too popular with his audiences and by the end of the year he was asking for more support in the form of subscribers but this did not materialise. Apart from this his concerts still remained popular with a large proportion of the concert going public. It also seems that the critics were pleased too as the response to the opening concert of the 1873-74 season was greeted with the words - "Mr De Jong, facile princeps on the flute, played his own well known Fantasia on Faust admirably". In the same month (October 25th 1873) he introduced his new song, "A Twilight Carol" with flute obbligato to words by the well known local poet Edwin Waugh. The newspaper critic noted "...a graceful and melodious composition with a flute obbligato which as played by the composer and the vocal portion expressively sung by Madame Rita, brought down the house and led to its repetition". On November 1st De Jong stepped in with a solo to cover for the indisposed Mme. Patey and once again received the admiration of a Manchester critic - "How Mr De Jong played his interpolated solo it is needless to say in a Manchester paper, his performance always possessing a uniform excellence". Damaré's piccolo solo on Airs from Lucrezia Borgia given a week later was encored and he was declared the best piccolo player Manchester audiences had ever heard. But the limelight for the flute and flautists of Mr De Jong's Popular Concerts was beginning to fade as the following year De Jong found it necessary to repeat his plea for more financial assistance in the printed programme for February 21st 1874. On the 27th the raising of funds continued with a Benefit Concert for which occasion the members of De Jong's orchestra kindly offered their gratuitous services and the Bands of the 7th Dragoon Guards and the 95th Regiment volunteered to take part along with thirteen soloists, choir and organist.

Although the Popular Concerts soon came to an end De Jong found it difficult to leave Manchester and the north and he continued to conduct concerts in the region at venues such as Buxton and Liverpool. He was just as successful at orchestral conducting as he was at playing the flute and composing for his instrument. In 1928 Macaulay Fitzgibbon remarked that in his hands "the flute almost became articulate . . . It literally sings, especially on the lower register". This can still be ascertained today when listening to his 1904 recording of "Auld Robin Gray" where his lovely ringing tone, firmly centred, shines through the surface noise of the disc.

He was then 69 years old, in very good health and recently married for the third time. Concert tours continued both in this country and abroad and one such tour in 1904 with Ben Davies (tenor) took him to Cape Town, S. A. He played professionally well into old age and enjoyed playing Briccialdi and Kuhlau duets. In later life he also took great delight in relating his experiences telling of having heard the famous Doppler brothers in concert.

Being so successful a musician it is no surprise that at that time during his career he would turn to teaching. The reason for this is usually twofold as generally speaking most musicians feel in some way obliged to pass on knowledge and experience to the next generation and it also helps earn a living. In 1893 De Jong joined the Royal Manchester College of Music staff as flute professor along with his colleague Firmin Brossa and was paid at the rate of 7/6d per hour. He remained in this post until 1906 when Vincent Needham, a pupil of both De Jong and Brossa, succeeded him. When one looks at De Jong's list of pupils it is very difficult to refute claims made for his expertise as a teacher; Vincent Needham, Albert Fransella (in c. 1875), A. Halstead, B. E. Samuels, and D. S. Wood were all to become eminent flautists of their time.

When Edward De Jong died on November 20th 1920 at Sulby, Isle of Man, aged 84, he was one of the last members of the original Hallé Orchestra to do so. He had started life on March 1st 1837 at Deventer in Holland first playing the flute in public when seven years old. At only 13 years of age he was sent to study at Cologne later moving to Leipzig to study his instrument with Hanke to whom he acted as deputy at the Leipzig Opera House. He was heard by Liszt who forwarded his career by introductions and it was said that he took part in early performances of 'Tannhäuser' and played obbligati to the singing of Jenny Lind. His first major orchestral appointment was in 1855 when after, according to Macaulay Fitzgibbon, he arrived in England "with one shilling and a sixpence in Dutch money in his pocket". From such meagre beginnings his career in England blossomed such that one Manchester critic was prompted to say that "Mr De Jong was a genius without eccentricities,unrivalled on the flute for many years and his power over an audience was immense".

Jean Firmin Brossa

J. F. BROSSA: 1871-1900

Jean Firmin Brossa (1839-1915) was 32 years of age when he arrived in Manchester from Paris to take up his appointment as principal and he remained for the following 29 years which is something of a record.

His early years are not very well documented but he was born in Geneva on 19th November 1839 and became a pupil of Vincent (Louis) Dorus at the Paris Conservatoire around 1860. Whilst in Paris he often performed with chamber groups playing, most notably, in quartets along with the celebrated French flautists, J. Donjon, Eugene Walckiers and Paul Taffanel. He moved to England in 1870 to take his place in Hallé's orchestra no doubt after having been highly recommended by one of Charles Hallé's Parisian contacts.

Life under Hallé's baton was no life of luxury. Programmes were long - some as long as three hours - and there was much new music to cope with. During the 1870's pieces by Wagner and Brahms made their first appearances at Manchester concerts and Hallé included much contemporary music too, such as Sterndale Bennett's G minor Symphony (Feb.18.1875), but Brossa found time to play in His Majesty's Opera too and tour with Mme. Albani in the USA and Canada as well as fitting in the usual seasonal work at Harrogate and seaside resorts.

Brossa began his tenure continuing the De Jong tradition in presenting flute solos to the public and on December 14th 1871, his first appearance as soloist, he played Demersseman's Fantasia on a melody by Chopin. The Manchester Evening News critic noted the following day that, "An interesting feature of the programme was the debut of Herr Brossa as a solo flautist in which capacity it would not have been easy to select a more suitable piece for the exercise of his undoubted taste and skill than Demersseman's Fantasie on a melody of Chopin. It afforded a most effective opportunity for displaying his admirable purity of tone".

At the close of his first season with the orchestra (1871-72), Brossa's colleague Oliver Gaggs (second flute) left the orchestra after having been a member for only one season and was replaced by William Henry Piddock who was a respected player and teacher, one of whose pupils was to become Hallé principal in later years. Henry Piddock remained for the rest of Brossa's 29 year tenure and during his first season with him witnessed Brossa's second appearance as soloist. Although there was to be less opportunity at Hallé Concerts for this kind of performance Brossa played another solo by Demersseman on January 18th 1872. Of his performance of the Fantasia in G (Il tremolo), the Manchester Evening News critic commented that, "Mons. Brossa as flute soloist more than sustained the high opinion which was formed of his ability on his recent appearance at these concerts. Demersseman's fantasia which he selected last night afforded ample scope for his wonderful powers of execution".

Brossa doesn't appear to have played any more solos of this type throughout his Hallé career but found opportunities now and again for chamber music such as Hummel's Septet in D minor given on Jan. 4th 1872 with Charles Hallé taking the piano part and section leaders (flute, oboe, viola, horn, cello and bass) taking the other parts. However, it was 22 years before Brossa appeared as a soloist in his own right at a Hallé Concert and this seems to have been primarily due to Hallé's programme planning rather than any unwillingness on Brossa's part. During the intervening period there was an upsurge in vocalists and violinists as soloists and Brossa was content to be a good and reliable section leader continuing to take part in many first Manchester performances. Bach's S. Matthew Passion - a work well known and loved by all flautists - was given on March 13th 1873 and two years later Grieg's Piano Concerto and Verdi's Requiem followed. At this time the Grieg concerto was only seven years old and the Requiem had first seen light of day only two years before.

In 1876 the flute section was increased in number to three. Brossa and

Fred Lax   © D.C. Miller Collection

Piddock were joined by Fred Lax (b.1858) as piccolo player who stayed for one season only. Lax was aged only 18 at this time but his name was already appearing to the forefront of British flautists. He was a well respected player who was a true soloist at heart and seeing no opportunity for his talents as such at Hallé Concerts decided not to stay with the orchestra. He toured extensively during the later years of the 19th century performing, amongst others, his own compositions many of which were based on traditional melodies. His wanderings took him to the United States where from the mid-1880's he performed as soloist with many famous bands including the Gilmore Band eventually settling in Baltimore in the early 1920's where his business card described him as being a composer, an arranger and a teacher of clarinet, flute, flageolet, saxophone and harmony as well as an agent for Bettoney Woodwind Instruments. He was also an early recording artist with the Stanzione and Finkelstein company for whom he recorded a performance of 'Lo, here the gentle lark' in 1908. He died in the late 1920's/early 30's leaving several solo pieces published by Cundy Bettoney of Boston and a Flute Method of some 287 pages published by Pepper & Son of Philadelphia.

When Lax left the orchestra in 1877, Brossa and Piddock remained and they were joined by Brossa's pupil, the young Vincent Needham who played piccolo with them for the next eight years. Great singers such as Albani and George Henschel, who later was to conduct the orchestra, appeared to much acclaim as Hallé's programmes excluded all instrumental soloists for a time in favour of vocalists engaged mainly to present oratorios.

On January 9th 1879 Brossa played in the first complete performance in England of Berlioz's Symphonie Fantastique and more works by Berlioz followed as a result of Charles Hallé's friendship with the composer. Hallé was then in his sixties but continued to seek out new works for his orchestra and of a performance of Berlioz's Romeo and Juliet at that time G. B. Shaw commented that in several passages there was "a ringing brightness of tone from the wind". Although Hallé returned to engaging instrumental soloists (Pachmann, Joachim, Piatti etc.) during the 1880's there was still no opportunity for Brossa to return as flute soloist but there were opportunities in new works presented by Hallé as on December 30th 1880 when he gave the first English performance of The Childhood of Christ with its marvellous trio for flutes and harp. Macaulay Fitzgibbon described Brossa as possessing "a wonderfully pure, delicate tone and a marvellous pianissimo", and one can well imagine him deploying these qualities at that performance. The programmes of the 1880's were varied, wide ranging and imaginative; so much so that no London concert programme at that time could measure up to those presented by Hallé in Manchester.

Charles Hallé succeeded Max Bruch as conductor of the Liverpool Philharmonic in 1833 and he ran these concerts concurrently with his Manchester series until his death in 1895. This meant of course that many of his players, including Brossa, performed at Liverpool, but they were used to travelling to venues outside Manchester as Hallé gave the Reid Concerts in Scotland (1868-1890) and he was conductor of the Bristol Festival too; and there was a winter season each year of two to five concerts a week spread all over Britain!

The flute section next saw a change of personnel in 1885 when L. F. Strelitskie arrived to replace Vincent Needham for three seasons after which Needham returned and embarked upon a rise through the ranks taking over from Brossa as principal twelve years later. Meanwhile in the late 1800's, Brossa was busy with changes other than personnel. The flute was still undergoing minor changes in design; changes mainly concerned with the key system in attempts to offer the flautists greater facility in fingering. Nowadays orchestral flautists may well be more concerned with alternative fingerings to cope with the demands of contemporary music but Brossa worked on and perfected an extra F# device rather like those found on Carte and Rockstro flutes. It appeared as an optional attachment to the Boehm system flute and became more popular than either the Carte or Rockstro device. It is actually a small touch key for use by the third finger of the right hand and is still found on many flutes in use today. Its action duplicated that of the third finger's regular key but unlike the regular F# key the small touch key can be kept down for producing E without covering the E hole. Its great advantage was in movement between E and F#. Thus it allowed the player to produce F# without depressing either the D or E key, it improved the F# through better venting and made it easier to trill E-F#. The year 1895 seems to be the earliest recorded sale of a flute with Brossa's F# key fitted, the work being carried out by Schumacher at Rudall Carte. Four years later Brossa's pupil, Lupton Whitelock, bought the first silver flute fitted with the F# mechanism and by the turn of the century his example was being followed by other well-known players, H. Warner Hollis and A. W. Arlom.

BROSSA'S F# KEY

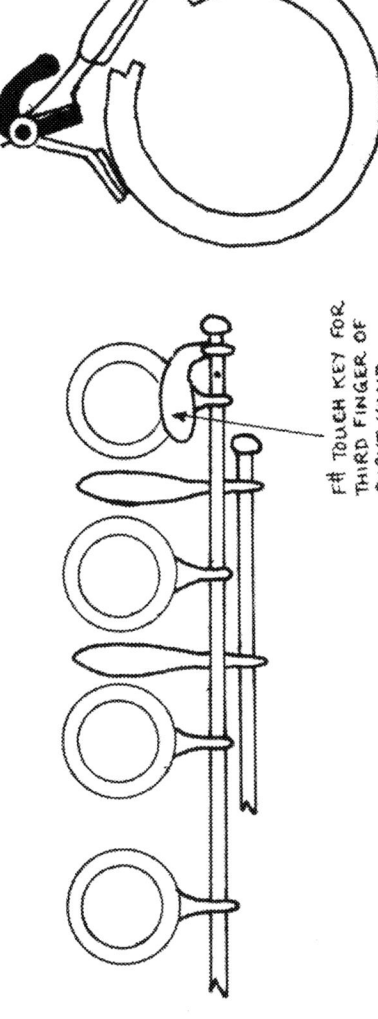

F# TOUCH KEY FOR THIRD FINGER OF RIGHT HAND.

THE SMALL TOUCH KEY DUPLICATES THE F# ACTION OF THE THIRD FINGER'S REGULAR KEY. ITS ADVANTAGE IS BETTER MOVEMENT BETWEEN E AND F#, AND BETTER VENTING.

The 1880's came to a close with Brossa continuing to give audiences orchestral solos such as those found in works like Grieg's Peer Gynt Suite (Jan.3rd 1899) and working with visiting composers presenting new works. Hamish McCunn directed the orchestra in his The Ship o'the Fiend Ballade at the last concert of the 1889 season and by the 1890's the orchestra had grown in size to 100 players or more. Visiting soloists included Paderewski and it may come as a surprise to some of us to learn that in the 1890's the orchestra still had an ophicleide player!

In 1893 the Manchester College of Music opened and Brossa was appointed Flute Professor being paid 7/6d per hour for his services. He had taken private pupils previous to this, Vincent Needham being the most well remembered of them, but there were others too who made good, notably Lupton Whitelock and Arthur Brooke. Brooke (1864-1950) studied with Brossa in the late 1890's, later emigrating to the U.S.A. where he was a member of the Boston Symphony Orchestra for nearly 30 years and conducted the Honolulu Symphony on occasion but still found time to make several transcriptions for four flutes, write a book of orchestral extracts, and around 1912 published a method for flute and 'Harmonic Fingerings'.

The following year work seems to have been a little more varied for Brossa as he appeared in a performance of the Adagio and Andante Quasi Allegretto in B flat from Beethoven's Prometheus music on 29th Nov. 1894. On that occasion solos for clarinet, bassoon, cello and harp were played by other section principals, Hoffman, Lalande, Vieuxtemps and Cockerill. Work with other organisations continued in 1895 when Simon Speelman, a viola player with the Hallé, ran a popular series of concerts beginning in October that year; Speelman conducted the orchestra consisting of Hallé members. There were also two opera companies active in Manchester at that time - Carl Rosa and the Rousbey Opera Companies - for whom Brossa undoubtedly played so the 1890's offered varied opportunities and plenty of work both in and out of Manchester.

By the time Brossa appeared again at a Hallé concert as a soloist in his own right William Henry Piddock had left the orchestra and Vincent Needham had returned as second flute. On Jan. 19 1899 Brossa had the responsibility of opening the Thursday concert with a performance of Bach's Suite No. 2 in B minor when the strings of the orchestra were conducted by Frederick H. Cowen. Bach's Suite was receiving its first Manchester performance and according to the Manchester Evening News critic, "Mr Brossa sustained his part admirably, and altogether the performance was a most delicate and dainty one". The Guardian critic however felt moved to write at greater length -

"Another most delightful feature of the concert was the Bach Suite for flute and strings which stood first in the programme. Each of the five movements given revealed some new phase of that wonderful old-world charm that belongs to the lighter compositions of Bach. We hope that there may have been among the listeners some of those who think of Bach as the driest of composers. If so they must surely have begun to reconsider that opinion in the first movement of the suite and finally rejected it when they heard that perfectly delightful Sarabande which was played yesterday by three single bow instruments together with the flute. The effect of tone colouring thus produced was quite different from anything we have heard before in the Free Trade Hall, and seemed as the exquisite imitative parts were woven together, to transport one back to the age when music was made 'apt for voices or viols', and noisy display had not yet become a feature of the art. The flute part which as in all Bach's music is rather unmercifully written as regards the performer's opportunities for fetching breath was admirably played throughout by Mr Brossa. We are not sure whether the use of single bow instruments in the sarabande instead of all the first violins, violas, and cellos was in accordance with Bach's intentions or was an idea of Mr Cowen's. In any case the effect was perfectly exquisite. It appeared from the programme that the suite was given for the 'First time at these concerts'; we hope not for the last time. At the end there was prolonged applause and our impression is that the audience wished to convey

THE HALLÉ CONCERTS.

Season 1898-99.

TWELFTH CONCERT,

Thursday, 19th January, 1899.

PROGRAMME.

Part 1.

SUITE FOR FLUTE AND STRINGS, in B minor -   *Bach.*
(First time at these Concerts.)

1. *Largo—Allegro.*   2. *Ronda.*   3. *Sarabande (Canon).*
6. *Menuet.*   7. *Badinerie.*

Flute - - - - Mr. F. Brossa.

CAVATINA - "Salve! dimora" *(Faust)* - - *Gounod.*

Mr. Ben Davies.

CONCERTO FOR PIANO, No. 5, in A - - - - *Mozart.*

Miss Margaret Pierrepont.

AN INTERVAL OF FIFTEEN MINUTES.

Part 2.

SYMPHONY, No. 3, in E flat—"EROICA" - *Beethoven.*

SONGS - - - { (a) "Feldeinsamkeit"
                 (b) "Die Mainacht"   } - - - *Brahms.*
                 (c) "Ständchen" - }

Mr. Ben Davies.

PIANO SOLOS - { (a) Prelude - - - - *Rachmaninoff.*
                 (b) Caprice - - - - *Scarlatti.*

Miss Margaret Pierrepont.

OVERTURE - - "Ruler of Spirits" - - - - *Weber.*

Conductor:

Mr. FREDERIC H. COWEN.

their special acknowledgements to the solo flautist as well as general acknowledgements to string players and conductor. But Mr. Brossa modestly declined to take any special credit to himself for his fine performance".

Brossa had waited a long time for the opportunity to give such a work at Hallé concert, the reasons for which are not exactly clear except as already noted, Charles Hallé's programme planning dictated the situation to a great extent and there was of course Brossa's modesty as noted by the Guardian critic, for he was certainly not the showman his predecessor was and in addition the tastes of the concert-going public were changing.

Brossa's last season with the orchestra saw him playing in a performance of Bach's St. Matthew Passion, a work he had helped introduce to Manchester audiences back in 1873 but now his colleagues in the flute section included two new members - W. Dixon and T. B. Marsden - whilst Needham continued to play second flute until the end of the season. Before joining the Hallé in 1899 Thomas B. Marsden had been active in London since the mid-1870's. He spent five years with the orchestra leaving in February 1904. During his time in Manchester he was also active as a teacher of flute and some years later his pupil William Thorn was to join the flute section. He also took on work outside manchester at the usual venues as well as at the Birmingham Festival (1903 etc) along with Dixon under Richter's direction.

Why Brossa chose to leave the orchestra in 1900 is not exactly clear but it is said that during a rehearsal of Beethoven's Overture Leonora No.3 the conductor asked that all the flutes play together the opening scale of G major (ascending from low D) as this passage was not easily heard when played on one flute alone. As principal, Brossa spoke up and argued the point that he wouldn't allow this as it was obvious that Beethoven had written the passage for solo flute. It is thought that this disagreement caused Brossa to resign his post soon afterwards. Unfortunately the Hallé programmes for Manchester concerts do not support the story as there was no performance of Beethoven's Leonora there during the 1890-1900 seasons. However, Frederick Cowen who was renowned for his Beethoven interpretations did present many of the composer's works during this period with the Hallé and in the 1899-1900 season Richter gave two of the symphonies along the Egmont Overture (16 Nov.1899). No doubt there were Beethoven performances at Liverpool and other venues given under the direction of Cowen and Richter so it is conceivable that such a disagreement might have occurred but the evidence is certainly not apparent.

Whatever the truth of the matter Hallé's death five years before had left the orchestra in a state of flux and perhaps Brossa considered it a good time to retire from orchestral playing anyway.

After leaving the orchestra in 1900 Brossa continued to play solos at concerts outside Manchester and was to be found in places such as Liverpool where in 1902 he played obbligato to a song by Altes at a Philharmonic Society concert. Four years later at the age of 67 he resigned his post as flute professor at the Manchester College of Music presumably retiring from most of his flute playing activities for the next eight or nine years until his death in 1915 at the age of 76.

His contribution to music making in the north of England had been lengthy showing great loyalty to the orchestra and also dedication to his pupils and the furtherance of the flute as a solo and orchestral instrument. It was fitting perhaps that he should relinquish both his orchestral post and his professorship to his worthy pupil Vincent Needham.

Vincent Needham   © Boosey and Hawkes

VINCENT NEEDHAM: 1900-1916

Richter is reputed to have said that Liverpool was a place of large ships and flute players and a number of players during his time with the Hallé actually came from that city. In 1900, although appointed principal flute in the Hallé, Vincent Needham still played in the Liverpool Philharmonic and continued teaching at the Liverpool College. He had been with the Hallé Orchestra since 1898 when he played third flute and piccolo becoming second flute the following year. In the year that he was appointed principal another Liverpudlian, E. S. Redfern joined the flute section as second, later to succeed Needham as principal after sixteen years, in circumstances other than he would have wished.

Born in Liverpool on April 15th 1856, Vincent Needham continued the now established line of Hallé flautists having studied under Edward de Jong and Firmin Brossa, and was no doubt proud to occupy the same position in the orchestra as his teachers had done before him. At the start of the 1900 season the usual stream of soloists appeared including Ysaye and Moritz Rosenthal. There was a performance of Belrioz's Faust on Nov.29th and Lady Hallé appeared on Dec. 6th giving Beethoven's Violin Concerto under Richter before the usual Messiah performance later in the month. Immediately after the Christmas break more soloists were billed including Siloti and Busoni and a concert was advertised for 24th January in which Vincent Needham was to play obbligato to Lillian Blauvelt singing Handel's Sweet Bird (Il Penseroso). However, the programme was changed at the last moment to include an Air by Handel and Ave Maria (Bach-Gounod) with violin obbligato played by the leader, Risegari. It wasn't long however before Needham's services were required as the originally advertised programme was given later that year on October 31st. The following day the Manchester Evening News critic was not too sure of Needham's abilities as accompanist writing, "In Handel's Sweet Bird she (Lillian Blauvelt) had the assistance of Mr Needham with a flute obbligato which was effectively played notwithstanding a little tendency to overpower the singer", but the

Manchester Guardian critic thought that "Handel's Sweet Bird was magnificently accompanied". This occasion was to be the first and last time Needham played flute obbligato to a singer in Hallé programmes and all subsequent appearances were in music by Bach. Songs and arias with obbligati were slowly disappearing from concert programmes.

October had been a busy month with a first Manchester performance of Elgar's Cockaigne (Oct. 24th 1901) and a flute obbligato to practise but the following month proved no less demanding with a performance of Bach's Mass in B minor on the 28th.

By the year 1903 Needham's reputation was such that he was in demand as an orchestral and solo flautist throughout the north of England and Richter took him to the Birmingham Festival that year along with his Hallé colleagues, E. S. Redfern, Fred Hatton, Thomas Marsden and W. Dixon. Their engagement at the festival continued in 1906 and 1909 and it was at one of these concerts that Richter first complimented Needham in public.

In February 1904 there was a change of personnel in the Hallé flute section when Fred Hatton who came from Liverpool like Needham and Redfern, took over from Thomas Marsden as third flute and piccolo player. He arrived just in time to appear in two performances of Elgar's Apostles (Feb. 25th & Nov. 10th) given by Richter whilst his colleagues Needham and Redfern continued their orchestral and soloist partnership with a first Manchester performance of Bach's Brandenburg Concerto No. 4 on December 1st 1904. "Brodsky gave a masterly rendering of the profuse and extremely animated violin solo; he was admirably supported by the flautists of the orchestra and the performance was of unqualified success". Again, the Evening News critic had slight reservations in writing, "The lovely Brandenburg Concerto was with the exception of the first few bars, delightfully given, the solo parts for violin and two flutes being played by Dr. Brodsky and Messrs. Needham and Redfern". This was the first in a

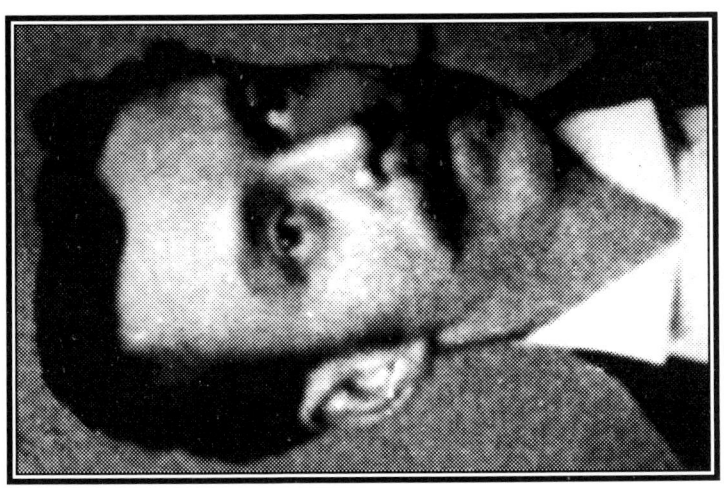

W.R. Dixon © Hallé

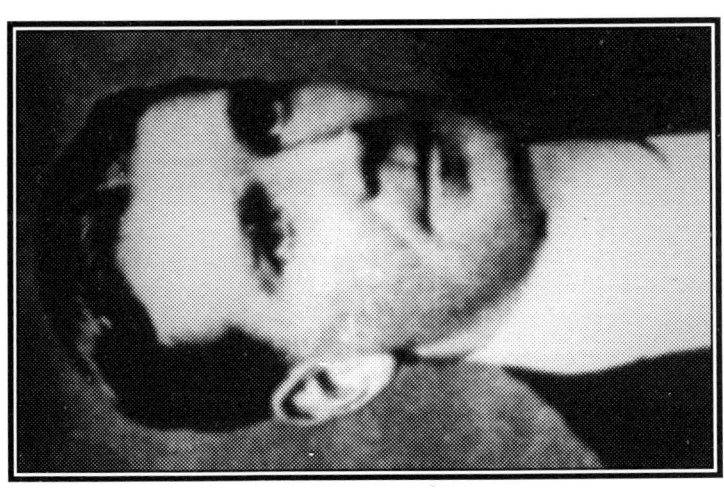

Fred Hatton © Hallé

31

series of Bach performances given by Needham which spanned the rest of his Hallé career. Indeed he seemed to have a special affinity with that composer's works as testified to by audiences and critics alike, and such performances were not confined to Manchester as in October 1910, with E. S. Redfern, he also gave the first Liverpool performance of Bach's Brandenburg No. 4.

Needham had first been involved in teaching at the Liverpool College but in 1906 he was appointed flute professor at the Royal Manchester College of Music in succession to his former teacher and colleague Jean Firmin Brossa. His pupils included J. Gilbert and Percy Whitaker. Gilbert was well known as principal flute of the North Pier Orchestra, Blackpool (where Needham also played on occasions) before emigrating to Australia and securing prominent positions in Adelaide, and Percy Whitaker eventually held important positions with British opera companies before becoming a member of the London Philharmonic Orchestra.

Needham's career of teacher, orchestral flautist and soloist continued quite happily during the early years of this century and on November 15th 1906 he appeared again at the Hallé concert in Manchester as soloist in Bach's Suite in B minor for flute and strings. This was only the second performance of the work in Manchester, (the first having been given by Brossa in 1899) and this occasion must have been one of the most memorable in Needham's career as ten years later the writer of his obituary in the Manchester Guardian made a point of mentioning it with the words - "perhaps his playing in the famous Suite of Bach in B minor when it was first given in Manchester under Dr. Richter showed his witty brilliance of style in a happier light than any music . . .". The day after the concert the Guardian critic announced that "The great success of the concert last night was undoubtedly Bach's Overture-suite in B minor for the strings and flute. It was we should think the best Bach playing we have heard in Manchester". He concluded with " and more delightful than all, how irresistible is the Badinerie that closes the

THE HALLÉ CONCERTS SOCIETY.

SEASON 1908-1909.

Executive Committee.

Mr. E. J. BROADFIELD, *Chairman.*

Mr. GUSTAV BEHRENS.   Mr. NEVILLE CLEGG.
Dr. ADOLPH BRODSKY.   Mr. C. COLLMANN.

Mr. J. AIKMAN FORSYTH, *Hon. Secretary,* 126, Deansgate, Manchester.

SEVENTEENTH CONCERT,

Thursday Evening, February 18th, 1909.

PROGRAMME.

Part I.

OVERTURE - - "Otello" (Op. 93) - - - - *Dvořák.*

CONCERTO, in D, No. 5 (" Brandenburg "), for
  PIANOFORTE, VIOLIN, and FLUTE, and String
  Orchestra - - - - - - - - - - - - - - - - - *Bach.*
Arranged by A. SILOTI.

Mr. SILOTI. Mr. RAWDON BRIGGS. Mr. V. L. NEEDHAM.

INTRODUCTION AND ALLEGRO for STRINGS - - *Elgar.*

PARAPHRASE for PIANOFORTE and ORCHESTRA—
  "Danse Macabre" *(Todtentanz)* - - - - - - *Liszt.*

Mr. A. SILOTI.

AN INTERVAL OF FIFTEEN MINUTES.

Part II.

SYMPHONY, No. 6, in F—" The Pastoral " (Op. 68)
                             —*Beethoven.*

Conductor - - Dr. HANS RICHTER.

Suite and was encored last night by Dr. Richter himself. The flute part was played exquisitely by Mr. V. L. Needham. What a delightful experience it must have been for him to play it - the reward for how much toil". For once the Evening News critic agreed with his colleague in writing, " It is necessary to say that the flute part played by Mr Needham was given with all the finish and purity of tone which characterises all his work". With this performance Needham had gained the renewed admiration and respect of his conductor, audience, fellow musicians and critics.

On 22nd October 1908 Debussy's L'après-midi d'un faune made its debut in Manchester programmes and Needham added the beautiful opening solo to his orchestral repertoire but it wasn't long before he was rehearsing the Bach Suite again for a performance in January 1909 to be followed quickly by another in March of that same year. The first of these performances on January 7th was conducted by Beidler and whilst there were doubts by both the Guardian and Evening News critics with regard to the strings, both agreed that Needham's part was a triumph. "Mr Needham was as usual thoroughly capable as solo flute" wrote the Evening News critic; and " . . . this movement (the Polonaise) was most excellently played by Mr Needham and both he and his colleagues achieved a triumph in the irresistible Badinerie".

A repeat performance given under Richter on March 18th was in aid of the Hallé Pension Fund and prompted the same critic to say that Needham played "with distinction" and that he was deservedly asked to acknowledge great applause.

NORTH PIER

BLACKPOOL

Secretary and Manager — JAS. WALKER.

Promenade Concerts

BY THE CELEBRATED

NORTH PIER ORCHESTRA

CONDUCTOR: PROF. SPEELMAN.

Programme—**Saturday, September 3rd, 1910.**

MORNING CONCERT AT 10-30.

1	OVERTURE	"Robespierre"	Litolff
		(An episode from the French Revolution.)	
2	ENTR'ACTE	"The Glow-worm" (by desire)	Paul Lincke
3	VALSE	"Kunstler Leben" (Op. 316)	Joh Strauss
4	POLKA for Two Piccolos	"The Two Little Finches"	Kling
		Messrs. NEEDHAM and WALKER.	
5	POLKA	"Buds"	Eilenberg
6	SELECTION	"La Reine de Saba"	Gounod

Interval of 15 Minutes.

7	OVERTURE	"Bohemian Girl" (English Edition)	Balfe
8	"Le Rouet de Grandmamau" (Grandmother's Spinning Wheel)		Gillet
9	GRAND MEDLEY	"Melodious Memories"	Herman Finch
10	VALSE	"Roses"	Eilenberg
11	MARCH	"Gringalet"	Ad. Gauwin

ADMISSION TO PIER, 2d.

The Open-Air Programme are subject to slight alterations.

35

Sandwiched in between these two performances Needham also took the solo part in Bach's Brandenburg Concerto No. 5 or rather Siloti's arrangement of it for flute, violin, piano and strings. Siloti took the piano part and Rawdon Briggs the violin part. The critics praised the arrangement but commented on Siloti's style of playing which was not always suitable for Bach. However, on the following day, Friday February 19th 1909 the Guardian critic proclaimed that "Mr Needham and Mr Rawdon Briggs both played excellently in their solo parts for flute and violin, and with close mutual understanding and concession that are essential". The Evening News critic joined in the praise saying that the performance was very beautiful and that "The slow movement was played by the solo instruments alone who kept an admirable balance of tone, and there was never the slightest tedium . . . The finale, resembling a dance, was delightfully played with much animation and there was loud and long continued applause at the conclusion".

But life wasn't all Bach for Needham although he had done much to help Dr. Richter to popularise his music with Manchester audiences. Other activities at this time included playing obbligato to Nellie Melba and of course the usual seasons of seaside Promenade Concerts often taking the opportunity to perform solos or duets with other great players of the day. On one such occasion, at the Saturday morning concert of September 3rd 1910 he appeared with Gordon Walker and the North Pier Orchestra, Blackpool, playing Kling's Polka for two piccolos - The Two Little Finches. Needham excelled in such pieces always being ready to show his prowess and more particularly his rapid tongue technique. According to Macaulay Fitzgibbon, on one such occasion a gentleman having just heard Needham produce his rapid double tongue expertise rose from his seat and walked round the stage to see if a second flautist was hidden behind the scenes!

After the summer season it was back to Manchester concerts with more new music in the form of Delius's Brigg Fair which was given for the first time in Manchester on November 9th 1911, and a concert of Elgar's music conducted by the composer followed a couple of weeks later.

Needham's final appearance at a Hallé Concert as soloist occurred two years later at a Thursday concert on December 4th 1913 when yet again Bach's Brandenburg Concerto No. 4 was the vehicle for the musicianship of Needham and Redfern, joined by Adolf Brodsky who also gave Elgar's Violin Concerto in the same concert. The Manchester Evening News critic noted that "Messrs. Needham and Redfern in the solo parts gave a period of healthy exuberance to the second part of the concert", and his colleague at the Guardia "admired the lightness with which this work was treated" and praised the conductor Michael Balling, for his "reduction of the strings and easeful treatment of this quite modest work".

At this time Needham and Redfern continued to appear together at other venues, most notably at Dr. Pyne's Town Hall Concerts and Sammy Langford, the Guardian critic, felt that Pyne's concerts had "certainly helped much towards completing the musical life of the city". Pyne's concerts were mainly of 18th century music which did not appear in the normal concert series in Manchester and in December 1914 Needham performed the Andantino from a Concerto in C for flute, harp and harpsichord and a Trio Sonata in E minor by Arne. Langford said that "Mr Needham the flautist, Mr Collier the harpist and Mr Foulds the cellist, all of the Hallé Orchestra, all played skillfully in the solo parts". A further item of interest at this concert was the Trio for two flutes and harp from 'Childhood of Christ' by Berlioz. For this piece Needham was joined by E. S. Redfern and Langford said that "it was an exotic on the programme and was the choice morsel of the concert".

The team of Needham and Redfern obviously worked well as these two flautists not only made a strong flute section in the orchestra but were often to be found performing as a duo.

In 1914 the Hallé flute section saw a further change of personnel when Fred Hatton relinquished his post to the young Joseph Lingard who was eventually to become principal. The flute section was now very strong indeed as all three men were good all round players capable of delivering the best in orchestral, chamber and solo work. One can well imagine the beautiful sound of their wooden flutes when they first delivered Ravel's Daphnis and Chloé Suite to a Manchester audience on 28th October 1915.

Almost exactly a year later on October 14th 1916 Vincent Needham died during a Hallé concert. Just before the interval a selection was given from Glinka's opera A Life for the Czar. Needham had just completed a prominent part in the selection and had risen to acknowledge the applause when he was seized with an attack of faintness. He was taken to an ante room and three doctors who were in the hall hurried to his help. On examination he was found to be dead. Sammy Langford wrote in the Guardian the next day that "some exquisite passages of arabesque for flute and clarinet were so perfectly played by Mr V. L. Needham and Mr Mills that they were personally called upon to acknowledge the applause but this very happy example of skill on his instrument proved to be the last of Mr Needham's long list of notable successes".

The concert continued after the interval with a performance of Greig's Peer Gynt Suite and in Langford's words, "few of the audience were aware that the peculiar reverence and intensity with which the beautiful lament for Asa's Death in the Peer Gynt Suite was played after the interval voiced for each player a sense of intimate personal loss".

Needham's career as a professional flautist spanned almost forty years and he held a most prominent position among flute players in the north of England. Indeed he was so far an acknowledged master of his instrument that this was recognised during his lifetime by colleagues, audiences, critics and authors. In 1928 he had been included in Macaulay Fitzgibbon's book, "The Story of the Flute" and throughout his career writers had noted nothing but praise for his artistic achievements. In Macaulay Fitzgibbon's words, "Needham was undoubtedly one of the finest and most effective orchestral flautists of the time".

A few days after the obituary appeared in the Guardian the first of two strange stories circulated in the form of a letter to the editor from Macaulay Fitzgibbon. Both stories however, related incidents of Needham's apparent nervousness before playing solos, although one finds this difficult to reconcile with his distinguished record as a soloist and orchestral principal. Fitzgibbon wrote that "on one occasion when I had the pleasure of playing along with Mr. Needham at a concert of the Dublin Philharmonic Society the overture to William Tell was included in the programme. As the famous flute passage drew near I observed that he was trembling violently. When it was finished and the concluding high G had died away into nothing he mopped away the perspiration which was standing out in beads on his forehead and remarked to me, 'I never come to that passage without shaking all over like an aspen leaf; if I made the slightest slip in it every single member of this large audience would notice my mistake'. One may explain this away by saying that any conscientious musician has passages or pieces that concern them more than others but the physical symptoms of Needham's concern don't always manifest themselves in such a dramatic way.

The second story relating to his apparent nervousness concerned his final concert and the day of his death. It is reported that Needham visited a cellist friend, also a Hallé member, on the day of his final concert in 1916 and told him that he was particularly apprehensive about that evening's concert when he was to play a solo in Glinka's Life for the Czar. His cellist friend thought it unusual that he should be troubled by such a solo. Needham played brilliantly that night of course, received much applause and died immediately afterwards.

The fact that his cellist friend thought it unusual for him to be troubled by solos leads us to suspect that Needham was not feeling himself that day and was a little concerned about his ability to perform well at the concert or maybe he had some kind of premonition of events about to unfold. Both stories provide a little intrigue perhaps but such nervousness would be remarkable in a player of his experience and standing. Without a full explanation available perhaps we shouldn't read too much into them. Whatever the truth of the matter it would not alter Needham's exemplary track record of being one of the great players of his day.

Edward Stanley Redfern

E. STANLEY REDFERN: 1916 - 1921

Following Vincent Needham's untimely and sudden death concerts continued to the end of the season with Edward Stanley Redfern in the principal's chair and this was now to become a permanent position for him for the next five years. He was a flautist of great talent and indeed the Redferns seem to have been a talented family altogether as not only was his father a professional flautist of some ability but his sister was remembered by Gerald Jackson in his autobiography as the female half of a Variety Theatre act, "Mr and Mrs Tom Mottramo", real name Mottram. As related elsewhere Redfern had joined the orchestra in 1900 and had been a very active and valued member. He had worked as a soloist with Needham and often took part in chamber concerts in the city.

Manchester however, was not his home town and he was proud of the fact that he was born in Liverpool - birthplace of other famous flautists Charles Nicholson and John Radcliffe. Teddy, as he was known to his colleagues, was born on 30th November 1866 and had studied the flute with his father Edward Beedon Redfern (1837-1893) who was known as one of the best flute players in the north of England and who had played with Jullien and in the Liverpool Philharmonic as well as theatre pits. The rest of his time was devoted to teaching as he ran his own flute school too. On his fifteenth birthday young Teddy Redfern gave his first solo concert in the St. George's Hall, Liverpool and obtained most favourable press notices. He had started flute studies and performed on an old system instrument but by the time he was nineteen he had changed to the Boehm system used today finding it difficult to cope with at first but in his own words, "soon found much more pleasure in it and I think I love the instrument more every day".

The first occasion on which he tasted life as an orchestral flautist was at the Old Amphitheatre in Liverpool where his father was engaged to play incidental music to Shakespeare's 'Tempest'. In Act II scene 3, the invisible Ariel plays on a tabor and pipe, and to produce this effect the flautist and a drummer had to go up into the roof space of the theatre and perform. One evening young Teddy went up in place of his father to play the piccolo part. The conductor was most concerned on seeing the elder Redfern still sitting in the pit at the appropriate moment and thought he had forgotten his cue until he heard the piccolo from above. Subsequently, the conductor, who had obviously enjoyed the joke had the young piccolo player brought to the theatre regularly for practice.

Many varied engagements followed and continued after he was appointed second flute in the Hallé Orchestra in 1900. He played under J. Riviere for a number of seasons, Speelman at Blackpool pier, Goossens and the Carl Rosa Opera Company in Liverpool and London and with George Henschel in the Scottish Orchestra for four seasons being with that orchestra when they were commanded to play before Queen Victoria at Windsor Castle. He also had a season with Dan Godfrey Jnr. at Bournemouth and played many solos with his band which resulted in Godfrey's father taking him on a tour of America and Canada playing solos at most of the concerts, receiving some very pleasing notices in the American newspapers. On this tour Teddy had played before President McKinley at the White House and travelled some 30,000 miles creating a sensation with his smooth sweet tone, admirable phrasing and phenomenal technique. As a token of appreciation he was presented with and used for a time, a gold flute made by Conn & Sons.

In spite of all this, in Redfern's eyes there was no higher honour than the position of principal flute for the Grand Opera season at Covent Garden. He held this position for several seasons before the First World War and was immensely proud of being able to succeed Radcliff as principal and to work alongside his much respected partners, H. Warner Hollis, W. O. Carrodus and Charles Souper. It is reported that at this time Redfern's exquisite playing of such passages as the scene of 'The Wandering Spirit' in Gluck's Orfeo often gained the admiration of the critics.

In 1916 when Redfern took over as Hallé principal the orchestra was almost entirely under the direction of Sir Thomas Beecham. Programmes changed quite drastically to include much recent and contemporary music. There were works by Delius, Strauss and Debussy added to which were numerous operatic pieces and while there were a number of outlets for singers the number of instrumental soloists declined. Ysaye, Moiseiwitsch and Busoni represented the big names in the list of soloists and apart from the odd violin solo from Arthur Catterall (leader) there were no soloists drawn from within the ranks during Redfern's tenure as principal flute so his reputation as a soloist hails from the days when he held the many coveted positions already mentioned. The opportunity for solo work with the Hallé did not present itself but no doubt there were many in his audiences who remembered his performances of Bach's Brandenburg Concerto No.4 with Vincent Needham in previous days.

Teddy Redfern's first concert as principal on October 26th 1916 was conducted by Eugene Goossens Jnr. who had taken over from Beecham at the last minute owing to the sudden death of Beecham's father and it contained a performance of Appalachia by Delius and Rimsky Korsakov's Sheherezade. The following month Elgar conducted a performance of Gerontius and in December Beecham gave the annual Messiah. In the New Year Beecham's presentation of a concert performance of Glinka's A Life for the Tsar on January 25th 1917 must have been a difficult occasion for all the players but especially so for Teddy Redfern whose thoughts on reaching certain solos must have been with his departed friend and colleague Vincent Needham. Before the season ended the sounds of Debussy's L'après-midi d'un faune came from Redfern's lips and at the same concert on March 1st 1917 Beecham conducted Petrouchka.

When the 1916-17 season ended Redfern and his colleagues found themselves with extra work as the orchestra was used for five weeks of

William Thorn   © Boosey & Hawkes

'Grand Opera in English' put on by Beecham in Manchester and including operas by Puccini, Verdi, Wagner, Mozart, Saint Saëns, Charpentier, Mussorgsky and Bizet - a marathon by anyone's standards! As well as taking on the job as principal Redfern had taken over Needham's professorship at the RMCM so life was certainly hectic.

The other two members of the flute section supporting Redfern in this arduous season were William Thorn and Joseph Lingard. Thorn (1878-1937) had joined in 1916 when Redfern became principal. He was a pupil of Thomas Marsden, who had also been a Hallé member, and had previously played in Blackpool Tower Circus Band and in the North Pier Orchestra where he had no doubt met Redfern on occasion. He gave 19 years service to the orchestra and both he and Lingard became the first Hallé flautists to broadcast for the BBC from Manchester in the 1920's. Thorn was also a member of the Liverpool Philharmonic and a teacher of flute at the RMCM.

The following season (1918-19) Beecham was still directing proceedings but Hamilton Harty arrived to give his own 'With the wild geese' on December 7th 1918 which was certainly new to the orchestra but Redfern was no stranger to the Bach B Minor Mass he presented on March 27th 1919. Over the next two seasons new works came fairly regularly into concert programmes - Albert Coates brought Skryabin's Poème de l'Exstase on November 8th 1919 with its mystical sounding chords supporting Redfern's solo flute at the opening. Cyril Scott was billed to appear in his first Piano Concerto (27th Nov) and more Skryabin on March 20th 1920 when the Divine Poem was first heard at a Hallé concert. Goossens presented John Ireland's The Forgotten Rite on December 16th 1920 and there was a chance for the wind players to appear in Beethoven's Rondino in E flat for wind instruments in the same concert.

In 1919 Redfern married for a second time but unfortunately the following year his personal and professional life was seriously interrupted by ill health and an unsuccessful operation for appendicitis. Adding to his problems was the fact that his new wife, his widowed daughter and grandson were all living with him and were dependent on him. This meant of course that he was often absent from the concert platform without pay making it difficult to manage. Needless to say, in his absence it fell to Joe Lingard to fill his place as he did on March 3rd 1921 in a performance of Bach's Brandenburg Concerto No.2 in F when the violin part was taken by Arthur Catterall and the other parts by section leaders.

However, there were memorable occasions even during that final period of illness. After a concert performance of Bizet's Carmen on Nov 6th 1920 conducted by Harty one critic noted that "few things more ravishing could be heard in music than the way in which Mr. Redfern's flute melody floated away from the accompanying harp in a certain movement from Carmen"; and friends were always ready to help where they could. A benefit concert on his behalf was organised and took place in the Shakespeare Theatre on the evening before his death. A sum of approximately £600 was raised and a further concert was arranged to take place at the Tower Theatre, New Brighton on Sunday October 30th 1921.

Edward Stanley Redfern died after a second operation at the Wallasey Cottage Hospital on October 10th 1921 and this date marked a rather sad and early end to the life of a remarkable flautist. He had had a very successful career and his art was recognised by royalty, heads of state, critics, friends and audiences alike. He had a large number of friends and was always willing to perform for them and would offer his services for any good cause. One writer noted his "most genial and kindly disposition" and the critic quoted earlier in writing of his performance in Bizet's Carmen also made reference to his character with the words, "a gentleness as lovely as the notes of this upward floating music is known to every player who ever acted as his colleague".

Like nearly all musicians Redfern had been involved in many first performances of music by composers we all come to know well and it would be wrong to associate him and his colleagues only with the display of Victorian trifles. At the same time it must be said that most flautists at the turn of the century were ready to display their technique using the many solos and obbligati of the day and some no doubt in a more musical way than others. Having held major positions in many of the well known British orchestras and opera companies Redfern's repertoire must have been immense but we are left, in the absence of recordings and living memories, with the impossible task of assessing his art. All we can do therefore, is to rely on reputation and career assessment and note one or two references which may point us in the right direction. Macaulay Fitzgibbon (The Story of the Flute, 1928) remembered him as possessing "a rich, smooth tone and remarkable technique" and the writer of his obituary in the Manchester Guardian on Tuesday October 11th 1921, stated that "Mr.Redfern had a refinement of style that was quite his own and something apart from

Joseph Lingard   © Boosey and Hawkes

mere dexterity on the instrument".

JOSEPH LINGARD: 1921-1934

When the Hallé season opened in 1921 Harty had done much to discipline the orchestra and develop a sense of style and Joseph Lingard had already had a taste of life as an orchestral principal having had to stand in for Redfern during his final period of ill health.

In the second concert of the season he was called upon to play the obbligato in Bishop's "Lo, here the gentle lark", a piece Redfern had no doubt played on many occasions during his distinguished career but never had the chance to do at a Hallé concert. The only critical comment came from the Manchester Evening News complaining that "some of the singer's high notes displayed a trace of unaccustomed hardness but she (Agnes Nicholls) managed to evoke considerable enthusiasm in Bishop's Here the Gentle Lark". No mention was made of the flautist!

After a fifteen minute interval Lingard launched into the complexities of Skryabin's Divine Poem with its trills and filigree work which was included in the second half of the concert conducted by Harty. He had seen this work only once the previous season when Coates gave the first Manchester performance but now he viewed it from a different chair and he no doubt realised that he had well and truly arrived at the position of principal flute. The position of second flute was now taken by J. F. Ridgway (d.1932) who was known as a perfect gentleman as well as a good flute player and William Thorn continued as piccolo player having already played alongside Lingard for five years or so and was to eventually put in nearly twenty years service seeing four principals come and go.

Born in 1880 Joseph Lingard was a pupil of William Henry Piddock and was already aged thirty four by the time he joined the orchestra in 1914 as piccolo player and third flute. He was made second flute two years

J.F. Ridgeway   © Boosey and Hawkes

THE HALLÉ CONCERTS SOCIETY.

SEASON 1923-1924.

SECOND CONCERT,

Thursday Evening, October 25th, 1923, at 7-30.

PROGRAMME.

Part I.

"THE MUSIC FOR THE ROYAL FIREWORKS"

—*Handel.*

(New transcription for modern orchestra, by *Hamilton Harty*.)

(First time in Manchester.)

RECIT. & ARIA—" Non mi dir " (*Don Giovanni*) - *Mozart.*

Miss DOROTHY SILK.

CONCERTO for FLUTE, HARP, AND ORCHESTRA - *Mozart.*

Solo Flute - - - - Mr. J. LINGARD.
Solo Harp - - - - Mr. C. COLLIER.
(First time at these Concerts.)

ARIA—" The Blessed Virgin's Expostulation " - - *Purcell.*

(When the Child Jesus tarried behind in Jerusalem.)

Miss DOROTHY SILK.

AN INTERVAL OF TEN MINUTES.

Part II.

TONE POEM—" EIN HELDENLEBEN " - *R. Strauss.*

Solo Violin - - - - - Mr. ARTHUR CATTERALL.

Conductor - - - Mr. HAMILTON HARTY.

later and had served under two great principals (Needham and Redfern) before becoming principal himself in 1921. He therefore had no illusions about what was expected of him and just as his predecessors had been he was also principal of the LIverpool Philharmonic where he appeared as soloist in Bach's Brandenburg Concerto No. 5 in the 1920's. In fact he still performed as an extra at Liverpool as late as the early 1950's.

In his first season as Hallé principal wind players were only represented as soloists by Lingard's own brief obbligato on Nov. 10th and Archie Camden's performance of Mozart's Bassoon Concerto in B flat on March 16th 1922. Harty was in the process of building up more interesting programmes and there were the usual illustrious guest soloists - Casals, Siloti, Busoni and Josef Hofmann amongst them. There was the Messiah in December and a performance of Bach's B minor Mass but to add variety a series of Hallé Operatic Concerts began on Jan. 14th 1922 with a performance of Bizet's Carmen. Joe Lingard concluded his first season as principal in a performance of Elgar's Apostles; so for the players the repertoire was rich and varied.

It wasn't until February 1st 1923 that Lingard was heard again as soloist. The work performed was Richter's arrangement of Bach's Suite in B minor which employs three flutes. Lingard took the solo part supported by his colleagues J. F. Ridgway and William Thorn. This work, in one form or another, had been a favourite with past Hallé principals and Lingard's performance did nothing to minimise its stature or popularity with the audience. Samuel Langford wrote in the Guardian the next day that "the main charm of the reading was in grace and subtlety and the three flautists who took part were loudly applauded at the close of the ravishing badinerie with which it ends". The Evening News critic agreed and added that it was "played with beautiful precision and taste".

The 1923-24 season was notable not only for the inclusion of some new works but also for the attainment of the 100th Hallé performance of Messiah. There was a performance of Vaughan Williams's Sea

Symphony and works by Bax and Moeran. Harty brought off a magnificent performance of Strauss's Alpine Symphony new to Hallé audiences and Lingard also introduced a new work to Hallé audiences in the form of Mozart's Concerto for Flute and Harp given with Charles Collier (harp) on Oct. 25th 1923. This performance gave the critics an opportunity to acknowledge the high standard of music making in the Hallé ranks, Lingard and Collier being referred to next day as two of the most gifted members of the orchestra revealing perfect mastery over their respective instruments.

However, perhaps the most notable concert of the season for Lingard was not his own performance of the Mozart concerto but the concert on Feb 7th 1924 in which Albert Fransella (1866-1934) gave the Mozart G major concerto for the first time at a Hallé concert. Although Lingard would be needed in the second movement where two flutes are employed in the orchestra, there is no doubt that he found plenty of time to observe his most illustrious colleague.

Fransella was a flute player of the first order for he was not just an accomplished technician but a musician to whom phrasing, tone and expression came naturally as a method of interpretation. He was especially admired for his skillful gradation of tone and he was of course a very experienced player having been a member of the Scottish, Crystal Palace, Royal Opera and Queen's Hall orchestras as well as a soloist and much respected teacher. His only tentative connection with the Hallé was that he had been a pupil of Edward de Jong's brother, Jacques.

On Feb 8th the Guardian carried a glowing report of his concert in which Sammy Langford said, "Mr Fransella's playing was notable first of all for the quality of its lightness and softness when these traits of fine playing were especially called for. It is a rare thing to have such lightness quite free from every sign of weakness as it was in Mr Fransella's playing. This delicacy lent a special charm to the cadenzas which Mr Fransella himself had written for the concerto, and which also had other interests of a constructional kind. That Mr Fransella's gift of lightness had its uses in Mozart's own music need not be said".

At the same concert Harty accompanied Fransella at the piano in his own Rhapsody: In Ireland, receiving its first Manchester performance for which the soloist shared a well earned triumph with the composer. According to the Guardian Fransella "revealed traits of great animation . . . especially at its close where Mr Harty's design seems to be that the instrument should burst itself a little. . . . its effect was of a freedom and gusto beyond our powers of hurried description".

For the rest of the season Lingard showed his expertise as principal in pieces such as Rimsky Korsakov's Flight of the Bumble Bee as well as the basic repertoire now expanded somewhat by Harty's efforts, and his music making outside the confines of the Hallé concerts saw a new departure for it was in 1924 that the BBC started making regular broadcasts. There were a number of flautists involved in early broadcasting from the Manchester/Northern Station including Harry Dobson, William Thorn, Frank O'Donnell, Arthur Redfern, John Crossley Hayes, Percival Anderton, Almena Marshall, Nancy Thirlwell, Ernest Fryer and Roy Richardson but Joe Lingard seems to have had his fair share of exposure on air. He made over 36 broadcasts between 1924 and 1934 many of which were solo recitals accompanied by Eric Fogg at the piano but there were other combinations too. He performed with other Hallé members such as Charles Collier (harp), Pat Ryan (clarinet), Stephen Whittaker (oboe) and J. F. Ridgway (flute) and with various singers. . His programmes show that in the 1920's Lingard was a busy chamber musician often appearing with Stephen Whittaker (ob), Harry Mortimer (cl), Otto Paersch (horn) and Archie Camden (Bassoon) as the Manchester Wind Quintet. Their programmes contained long lists of composers now almost forgotten but certainly ignored by present day music makers. There were pieces by Sobek, Onslow, Val Hamm, Pessard, Kronke, Ilsa, Revell, Colomer, Brumer, Akimenko and many more. Flautists today might recognise the name of Paggi whose Fantasia:

Neapolitan Memories Lingard broadcast several times between 1927 and 1937 in Edward de Jong's arrangement, and also the Briccialdi Brilliant Duets, one of which he broadcast on August 8th 1927 with his Hallé colleague J. F. Ridgway.

By the end of the 1920's the Manchester Wind Quintet had changed its name to the Northern Wind Quintet for which Alec Whittaker played oboe and Pat Ryan (cl) took the place of Harry Mortimer but within the next few years the Hallé Woodwind Quartet was formed with Lingard as flautist along with Fred Tilsley (ob), Harry Mortimer (cl), Maurice Whittaker (bassoon) and Eric Fogg (piano) giving a performance of Eric Fogg's Quintet on 25th Feb 1934.

A broadcast of Harty's "In Ireland", with the composer at the piano in a St. Patrick's Day programme in 1929, must have jogged Lingard's memory of having heard Fransella play the piece four or five years before in the Hallé series and leaves one wondering which of the two flautists managed to suggest the alternations of tragic wildness and gay insouciance more strongly, as the flute part contains a certain amount of virtuosity.

Although busy as a chamber musician in the 1920's Lingard was not idle as a soloist either as there were two appearances at Hallé Concerts in the 1924-25 season. On March 5th 1925 Richter's arrangement of Bach's Suite in B minor was brought out again with the assistance of his colleagues J. F. Ridgway and William Thorn and a fortnight later on March 19th he played Godard's Suite for flute and orchestra presenting it for the first time in Manchester at the last concert of the season. The Bach flute works never failed to please critics or audiences in Manchester and once again the notice in the Evening News was favourable - "Bach's overture for flute and strings was deliciously played, the three flautists concerned being the recipients of very cordial acknowledgement".

The following season (1925-6) there was a change of personnel in the flute section when J. F. Ridgway left the orchestra after five years service

Norman Seville   © Clifford Seville

and thirty six year old Norman Seville took his place. Born in 1889 Seville studied at the Royal Manchester College of Music with Vincent Needham and Teddy Redfern and like his masters, played on a Rudall Carte wood flute with silver keys. He first played with the Hallé as deputy before the First World War but after his demobilisation from the West Yorkshire Regiment in 1924 he joined the Hallé as piccolo player. He stayed with the orchestra about 18 years or so and during that time involved himself in various other ventures such as the summer seasons at the seaside towns. For many years he played in the Spa Orchestra at Scarborough under Alick Maclean along with Charles Collier (harp), Ted Stansfield (Gracie Field's uncle) and later Vernon Harris. By the early 1940's the BBC Northern Orchestra had become a permanent orchestra and players could no longer be involved with two orchestras. They had to choose either the Hallé or the BBC and so it was that a number of players including Norman Seville decided to join the BBC as full time members. Seville stayed with the BBC until his retirement in the 1950's spending his last years in Seaford, East Sussex where he died in 1968.

During the 1925-26 season Harty widened the orchestra's repertoire considerably. Works by Bartok, Respighi, Bax, Ravel, Elgar, Vaughan Williams and Sibelius featured in the concert series and Manchester heard for the first time Berlioz's Grande Messe des Morts. Joe Lingard's contribution was not so much as soloist but he continued to carry out his duties as principal most notably in works such as Debussy's L'après-midi (Dec 10th 1925) and Holst's Fugal Concerto (Jan 7th 1926) with the oboist Alec Whittaker. Samuel Langford found the new work not altogether convincing - "The Concerto was given in a very delicate and refined manner which gave it the fascination of a miniature but the absolute fidelity of which to the composer's intentions we somewhat doubt". No mention was made of the soloists.

The following season the flute section was maintained at four in number and Keith Whittaker joined staying for two seasons only. He was a pupil of Norman Seville at the Royal Manchester College of Music where he studied on a Candlin Wind Scholarship 1920-23. He was an excellent piccolo and alto flute player and spent some years before the Second World War with the BBC Symphony Orchestra but his life ended in tragedy, being found dead on Hampstead Heath.

For Joe Lingard preparations were well under way for his next solo appearance scheduled for Oct. 28th 1926 when he was to perform Bach's Brandenburg Concerto No.5 in D with Harty at the piano and Alfred Barker on violin. Vincent Needham had given the first Manchester performance of this work in February 1909 to great acclaim and the Guardian critic was not too disappointed on this occasion either -" . . . light hearted happiness was unfolded in the delicious concerto of Bach! . . . and both Mr Lingard with his flute and Mr Alfred Barker with his violin had a sort of heavenly employment in the music too. Mr John Bridge was a judicious conductor who held this light music with an easy rein, and did nothing whatever to mar its freedom and ease". The Bach performance was to be Lingard's last appearance as soloist in the Hallé Concert Series but there was much work being done in another direction. Both Lingard and his colleague William Thorn were now heavily involved again in early broadcasting from Manchester.

In 1928 J. F. Ridgway returned to take over from Keith Whittaker for two seasons and at the end of that time he was replaced in turn by one of Joe Lingard's star pupils, the young Geoffrey Gilbert who also remained as third flute for a further two seasons until 1933 when the flute section was down to three in number and stayed as such for some years to come. From 1929 onwards the remaining years of Lingard's tenure as principal were arduous enough judging by the number of new works being presented by Harty which included Mahler's 9th Symphony and Shostakovich's Symphony No.1 Op.10. Added to these, numerous British works were receiving attention and there were smaller but no less demanding works already in the repertoire. It is indeed fortunate that Harty's attention was directed towards recording with his orchestra as in 1929 a 78rpm recording of Rimsky Korsakov's Flight of the Bumble Bee appeared, thus giving us a chance to hear for ourselves the precision fingering and total control exhibited by Lingard on that occasion. Even through the surface noise of that old disc his performance can be followed note for note! His tone is large and his technique flawless. It is difficult to decide where if anywhere, he breathed!

By 1930 Lingard's career had developed from orchestral flautist into that of principal, recording artist, broadcaster, chamber musician, recitalist and respected teacher but in 1934 he ceased to be Hallé principal, relinquishing his post to his pupil Geoffrey Gilbert who took his place for one season only before Beecham took him to the London Philharmonic which he had recently formed. But activity for Lingard did not cease there, for on Nov 5th 1936 he performed Bach's Brandenburg Concerto No.5 with the Hallé under Sir Henry Wood in a BBC broadcast, and other such appearances continued until 1937 when he rejoined the Hallé as second flute, remaining until 1948.

After he had retired from Hallé and other professional playing in the 1950's, Joe Lingard played as an extra with the Yorkshire Symphony Orchestra, but by 1955 he had lost the use of his fingers on the left hand. In a letter to Geoffrey Book dated that same year he wrote that he had "been to a specialist and had 'electric massage' twice a week which didn't improve things". His playing days were over but he maintained his good sense of humour and in the final lines of the letter he appeared contented with his achievements in life in writing, "Oh well, I suppose I've had a good innings". A good innings indeed, for he died in 1969 at the age of 89 after having spent forty years as a professional.

In taking over as Hallé principal from Teddy Redfern in 1921, Joe Lingard had also taken over Redfern's teaching duties at the Royal Manchester College of Music and over many years was responsible for the training of many excellent flautists. Among his list of pupils can be found the name of Oliver Bannister who eventually became Hallé principal himself in 1945. Lingard's pupils remember him with affection and respect and seem to agree that he was a straight person and a gentleman. He was the most modest and generous of men who always wanted to give credit to his students who had done well, and his common sense approach to teaching emphasised the practice of long notes, basic scale exercises, chromatic exercises, scales in intervals and an exercise of his own invention - that of arpeggios decorated with turns. Favoured pieces were the Bach Flute Sonatas and the Konzertstück Op.98 by Heinrich Hofmann (1842-1902) for flute and string orchestra. He used a vast amount of orchestral extracts compiled from the repertoire by himself, and his pupils had to copy them out before practising them. Part of every lesson was devoted to duets and trios, and although Lingard seldom demonstrated during lessons he would always take part in trios or duets, using his straight well centred sound without a hint of vibrato.

His open-mindedness and tolerance towards his pupils is apparent when one considers that as a student, Oliver Bannister admired the French flautists and was attempting to use a more flexible approach to his own playing, and even though his teacher left him in no doubt that he did not approve, he was not prevented from proceeding. Joe Lingard was forthright and a man of few words, but his kindness and generosity towards his pupils and others was always clearly intimated.

Geoffrey Gilbert   © Boosey and Hawkes

GEOFFREY GILBERT: 1934-1935

When Geoffrey Gilbert died at the age of 74, The Times (22nd May 1989) described him as "the most influential British flautist of the twentieth century".

He was a prominent teacher and performer who helped considerably with the adoption of French style flute playing by English flautists through his prominence in the orchestral community and teaching establishments during the period before the Second World War when he decided to change from wooden to silver flute.

In addition to holding appointments with major orchestras under the great conductors, Gilbert premiered in England many of the most important flute concertos of the twentieth century including those by Ibert, Nielsen, Jolivet and Rivier.

Born to Welsh parents in Liverpool on 28th May 1914, Gilbert's first musical activities began at the age of six on the tin whistle, encouraged by his father who played the oboe in a music hall orchestra. He soon took up a simple system piccolo, and whilst on holiday at Kirk Michael in the Isle of Man he gave his first performance on that instrument, playing 'The Mocking Bird' by Frank Brockett.

At the age of twelve, serious flute studies began with Vincent Needham (Jnr) whose father of course was Vincent L. Needham, Hallé principal 1900-1916. Needham (Jnr) taught from a method handed down from his father, and was an orchestral player himself. He often played for a silent cinema in Birkenhead and encouraged Gilbert to join in reading with the orchestra there. Thus, valuable experience was gained and Gilbert was soon offered his own job at another cinema, but being under age he was not allowed to take up the position until special dispensation was given by the union.

A scholarship to study at the Liverpool College of music took him to his next teacher, Albert Cunnington who worked mainly on tone quality, and Gilbert's musical experiences came through amateur societies, the David Lewis Military Band and occasional cinema jobs. It was to be his cinema jobs that enabled him to pay for tuition at the Royal Manchester College of music which he entered on scholarship to study with Joseph Lingard who was then Hallé principal. Like his earlier teachers, Lingard had an incredible technique and his extensive technical work with Gilbert coupled with the cinema jobs enabled him to become an excellent sight reader at an early age. Even as student in 1930 Gilbert caught the attention of the critics. When he performed the Chaminade Concertino Neville Cardus wrote - "Mr Gilbert drew so much winsome melody out of his flute and so much that was piquant in phrase and rhythm".

Student life was busy, as two or three times a week he would travel to Manchester by train in time for a class at 9am, spend all day in lessons, orchestra or ensemble classes, catch the 4.30 train back to Liverpool to be at the cinema by 6.30 and then go home afterwards to begin practice. After three years of study with Lingard at the RNCM, Gilbert secured his first position in a military band in Southport, and by the age of sixteen he was playing flute in the Hallé orchestra along with his teacher under Harty. In later years Gilbert commented that "although at first he (Harty) seemed rather austere and sometimes frightening with his volatile Irish changes of humour, I thought he was the finest orchestral trainer I ever encountered and I believe I learned more from him and the older members of that fine orchestra during this period than at any other time in my orchestral career". No doubt Gilbert learned much from his colleagues in the flute section - William Thorn and Norman Seville, who had already been members of the orchestra for some years and continued for several more years after Gilbert had left. Within four years of joining the Hallé, Gilbert became principal succeeding Joe Lingard, and of course similar positions with the Liverpool Philharmonic and BBC Northern Orchestra went along with the job, as at this time Hallé players were also members of these other two orchestras.

In 1933 Harty resigned his Hallé conductorship and the orchestra was left in a state of disarray, with Beecham trying to coordinate things. Even the usual Messiah performances were dropped through financial difficulties and programmes were not very adventurous. The 1934-35 season did not prove to be a very remarkable one from the point of view of programme planning, but apart from Beecham's presentations there were visits from Barbirolli, Sargent and Malko. Sargent gave the Bach B minor Mass on Jan 24th 1935, giving the flute section something to think about, but there were no openings for solo flautists, so Gilbert took the opportunity of taking part in Bach's Brandenburg No. 4 at Liverpool in the same month, following in the footsteps of his predecessors, Brossa, Needham and Redfern.

Gilbert's friendly association with Beecham at this time led to Beecham securing his services for his London Philharmonic Orchestra and at nineteen Gilbert was a principal of this great body of musicians, a position he held until 1939. At the beginning of his London career he held the Hallé and Liverpool posts simultaneously, which involved much travel between the three cities. During his years with the LPO Gilbert heard the French flautists Marcel Moyse and Rene le Roy, and decided that he must adopt the French style of playing if he was to produce similar warmth and expression in his sound. Eugene Goosens introduced him to Rene le Roy and he had lessons with him when he visited London. He was advised to change his embouchure and articulation, learn to use vibrato properly and buy a new instrument which he did. He bought a Louis Lot silver flute and attempted to relax his embouchure. He worked on articulation and breath support to make the sound vibrate, and it took nearly three years of hard work to perfect.

The Second World War brought orchestral duties to an end and Gilbert served for a time in the Coldstream Guards Band, and life wasn't quite so pleasant as it once had been but there was time towards the end of his service for more practice and in 1946 he returned to music and the LPO. He resumed teaching, now advocating the French style and influenced many flautists, teachers and students through his positions on the staffs of Trinity College of Music (1947-65), Guildhall School of Music (1948-69), and the Royal Manchester College of Music (1957-69).

In 1948 Geoffrey Gilbert became principal of the BBC Symphony Orchestra and was also busy at this time founding the Wigmore Ensemble along with other principals of London orchestras. The ensemble was very successful and flourished for twenty one years or so, appearing at festivals and making numerous broadcasts. There were solo engagements too at which Gilbert presented many premieres and revivals of concertos and chamber music by Getry, Bach, Haydn, Pergolesi and Gluck among others. He stayed with the BBC for four years (1948-52) and during this period he was still interested in experimenting with different flutes. He purchased and performed for a while on the only platinum flute in England at that time.

Being very well respected by all musicians gave Gilbert the chance to choose his career path from now on, and in 1957 he continued his teaching by taking over from Peter Lloyd as Flute Professor at the Royal Manchester College of Music and joining Beecham again in the Royal Philharmonic Orchestra where he remained until 1963, but he still maintained solo engagements managing to return to Liverpool in May 1959 giving a performance of Luigi Nono's Y Su Sangre. The following year Eugene Ormandy offered him the position of principal flute with the Philadelphia Orchestra but he was unable to take up the position as he was not an American citizen, and on the death of Sir Thomas Beecham in 1961 he decided that "after the loss of Sir Thomas from the musical world I no longer felt that I wanted to be a regular member of a symphony orchestra except perhaps an odd performance as a guest artist". Such was the influence of Beecham on Geoffrey Gilbert the orchestral player and friend.

Most of his energy from this point on was directed towards teaching, and as RNCM staff member he conducted wind orchestras and the Training Orchestra which he formed at the college in September 1966.

Offers from overseas however were still coming in and Geoffrey eventually left England with his wife in 1969 to take up a Professorship at Stetson University in DeLand, Florida. For the next ten years he was Director of Instrumental Studies and Conductor in Residence there, and on retirement from that post in 1979 he took private pupils and gave masterclasses. The next ten years were extremely busy and his masterclasses took him to all parts of the United States as well as Canada, England, Germany, Holland and Ireland. It was after more than one successful career, on May 18th 1989, that Gilbert died at his home in Florida, and in the Guardian on Saturday May 20th William Bennett was prompted to write - "In his fifties he moved to America to teach and subsequently toured world wide . . . This second career proved as astonishing as his playing career had been. A brilliant and progressive professor, his ability to bring out the best in every individual musician and his sparkling sense of fun have left a host of grateful pupils all over the world". Indeed his list of distinguished pupils is long, including James Galway and two flautists who were to become Hallé members themselves - Douglas Townshend and Francis Nolan.

Geoffrey Gilbert's influence is now being felt world wide through succeeding generations of flautists and his importance as a teacher is being fully realised.

Vernon Harris　　　© Boosey and Hawkes

VERNON HARRIS AND
ARLISS MARRIOTT: 1935-1945

Towards the end of the 1935-36 season and at the beginning of the next, it was apparent to everyone that things were not the same as they had been under Harty's direction, and in spite of only a few changes in personnel since 1933 the orchestra was lacking in style and had lost its sparkle through a constant stream of guest conductors and poor programme planning.

Some changes in personnel were supervised by Beecham who lured Geoffrey Gilbert to London and brought in Vernon Harris as the Hallé's principal flute in 1935. Of course at this time the Liverpool and BBC jobs came along with the Hallé job, so the position was a very responsible one. His colleagues in the flute section remained the same as under the previous two principals, with Norman Seville playing second and Billy Thorn piccolo.

Born in 1898 and a pupil of past principal Vincent Needham, Vernon Harris had served his apprenticeship in the traditional way, playing on a Rudall Carte wooden flute, spending winter seasons at Hastings, summer seasons at Harrogate and later with Alick Maclean and his Spa Orchestra at Scarborough where he played second to Norman Seville. He became a professional flute player in the 1920's after having served a seven year apprenticeship in engineering, and although adequately fitted for the role of principal flute his task in that first season with the Hallé was difficult enough, considering the general state of things. However, he had the opportunity of observing Horowitz and Rachmaninov at close quarters, and the season passed uneventfully into the next when he got the chance to perform Bach's Brandenburg Concerto No.5 in D with Alfred Barker (leader) and Myra Hess under Henry Wood's direction on Nov. 5th 1936. The Guardian critic wrote that "The Fifth Brandenburg Concerto of Bach was delightfully given .

. . Mr Vernon Harris and Mr Alfred Barker took the flute and violin solo parts respectively and with Miss Hess as pianist the interpretation was clear and firm". Another critic agreed, saying that they gave a "concise and firm reading of the work" but (remembering that writers were not too well disposed towards the orchestra at this time) he was left with a feeling of dissatisfaction at the end of the performance, blaming mainly Bach's monotonous writing and hoped that it would be at least another ten years before the Hallé played it again!

The soloists, however, came out of it unscathed, and the remainder of the season was notable only for the fact that Vernon Harris played the beautiful solo in Debussy's L'après-midi for the first time with the orchestra on Oct. 15th 1936 under Pierre Monteux. This piece was performed so often during the late 1930's and early 1940's that of all Hallé principals Vernon Harris must hold the record for delivering that solo, in which he was able to demonstrate the characteristic limpid sound quality and controlled vibrato only he could produce in such pieces.

Programmes given by Sargent and Beecham in the 1937-38 season were a little more interesting, and included a performance of Berlioz's Childhood of Christ on Feb. 25th in which Harris and Seville delivered the delightful trio accompanied by the harp. At the end of the season Billy Thorn left the orchestra after twenty-one years spent mostly as piccolo player, and was replaced by Joe Lingard who returned as second flute, leaving Norman Seville to play piccolo, but at the outbreak of war in 1939 the orchestra was beset by more problems when the Free Trade Hall was taken over and used as a store, and public assemblies at places of entertainment were banned. This meant taking up residence at the Paramount Cinema (later the Odeon) in Oxford Street, giving Sunday afternoon concerts, and the following year involved much travel to places such as Wrexham, Blackburn, Bolton, Stockport, St. Helens, Rochdale, Nelson, Oldham, Hanley, Barrow and Ulverston.

For the 1941-42 season The Opera House on Quay Street became the

Hallé's temporary home, and Malcolm Sargent was firmly established as Conductor-in-chief. In the summer there were concerts at the Tower, Blackpool but on Sunday Sept. 21st 1941 Sargent gave a concert at the Pier Pavillion, Llandudno in which he featured Vaughan Williams's Greensleeves Fantasia, the opening solo beautifully delivered by Vernon Harris, as can be heard in the recording made for HMV shortly after this concert. The Intermezzo from Delius's Hassan was also recorded about the same time (1942) with Constant Lambert conducting, and although the quality of these recordings leaves much to be desired by modern standards there is enough to determine that Vernon Harris was a very fine player with a good technique and a lovely sound. As mentioned in previous pages, British flute players held on to their wooden flutes and associated sound long after their European colleagues had abandoned them for metal ones, and Vernon Harris was no exception, but he did experiment with different headjoints in search of easier production of his personal sound quality.

By the summer of 1942 audiences had increased, and for the first time players were not thinking of going to their usual seaside resorts for the season but remained together for further concerts, visiting London and Chester with great success, although nearly twenty members were still away in the forces. Problems in co-operation with the BBC, who were reluctant to release players for the extra Hallé commitments, and developments in Liverpool, pointed to the formation of three separate fully professional orchestras in the north of England - the Hallé, Liverpool Philharmonic and BBC Northern Orchestras. The following year Hallé players were offered a yearly contract (200 concerts per year) and members of the orchestra who also played for the BBC were asked to declare their allegiance. Thirty one members of the orchestra decided that the security of life with the BBC was preferable to the uncertainty offered by the Hallé, and it was then that the Hallé flute section underwent considerable change with the departure of both Vernon Harris and Norman Seville, leaving stalwart Joe Lingard to cope with new colleagues alone.

Before Harris left there were more new works to get to grips with, and several more performances of Debussy's L'après-midi, but his swan song as soloist came with the chance to play Bach's Brandenburg Concerto No.5 again with Myra Hess and Laurance Turner on March 1st 1942 in an afternoon concert at the Opera House conducted by Leslie Heward. The following day the Manchester Evening News carried no report of the concert, but the Guardian critic admitted that "the flute and the violin solos played respectively by Mr Vernon Harris and Mr Laurance Turner have an important place in the scheme", but went on to write about the dominating influence of the piano and Leslie Heward's achievements of late. It appears that critics had lost interest in flute players, along with the public who now only had eyes and ears for virtuoso pianists. There was a general disenchantment with the orchestra's achievements but it does lead one to suspect that critics no longer knew what to look for in a wind player and only felt obliged to comment on those aspects of the concert which they knew had popular appeal. Thus, Vernon Harris's last appearance as soloist at Hallé concerts passed almost unnoticed. Little wonder that in these unsettled times he decided to leave the orchestra the following year for new adventures with the BBC, lasting until 1951.

During his period with the BBC, Vernon Harris would often stand in for Joe Lingard at the RNCM when the latter was prevented from taking up his teaching duties through other commitments, and most of the lesson time would be taken up with looking at orchestral repertoire in great detail. Of one such occasion Joan Simpkin, a Lingard pupil, has written, "With the studies propped up on the stand, Vernon would appear, take one look at them and then say, 'Oh, I don't think we'll have those today - let's have a bit of Debussy' (pronounced Di-busy) and would launch into L'après-midi or Syrinx, then realising there was no music for these, he would return forlornly to the studies". Following his departure from the BBC in 1951, a long period of ill health prevented Harris from taking on such demanding work as principal flute, but he did manage the odd season at Bridlington before his death in 1966.

Arliss Marriott

© Jane Morse

With the reorganisation of the orchestra and the changes of personnel in 1943, Joe Lingard had been left to receive a new principal and second flute. They were Arliss Marriott and Oliver Bannister, who was to be such an asset to the Hallé wind section in the years to follow. The story of Barbirolli's fortuitous return to England from America and his reconstitution of the orchestra has been well documented elsewhere, but his first Manchester programme on August 15th 1943 included Vernon Harris's favourite L'après-midi solo performed by the new principal Arliss Marriott, and one critic was pleased to write - "The orchestral playing was indeed finer than any we have heard in Manchester for many years . . .".

Arliss Marriott, known as Bill to his colleagues, was already an experienced player and teacher before he arrived at the Hallé. Born in the 1890's and a pupil of the famous Robert Murchie he was well known in London as a member of the Old Vic and Sadler's Wells Orchestras, and during the 1930's was professor of flute at Rodean School. Other activities included much chamber music playing, and it was also in the 1930's that he founded and played as leader of The English Wind Players' Quintet, performing mainly in the south of England. Before 1942 he had been principal flute of the BBC Scottish Orchestra, but moved back to London for the 1942-43 season, playing second flute with the London Philharmonic Orchestra before coming north again to take up the Hallé position. Apart from L'après-midi at the beginning of his first season with the orchestra there were other important pieces to cope with, such as Ravel's Daphnis and Chloé on Oct. 3rd 1943, but the following year Bach's Brandenburg Concerto No.4 was brought out again with Bill Marriott and Oliver Bannister performing it on three successive days (14th, 15th, 16th Jan 1944) in Sheffield, Bradford and Manchester to much acclaim, and then again the following month at Hanley. This was the only chance Hallé audiences had of hearing Bill Marriott as soloist, but according to the Guardian critic writing of the Manchester performance on the 17th, everyone was pleased - " . . . it was during the performance of the Fourth Brandenburg Concerto that

NEXT CONCERT—

LONGFORD THEATRE :: STRETFORD

Sunday, January 16th, 1944, at 2-30 p.m.

Brandenburg Concerto No. 4 for Two Flutes, Violin and Strings . *Bach*

Symphony No. 1 in C . . . . . *Beethoven*

Suite from the Incidental Music, Pelleas and Melisande . *Faure*
(first time in Manchester)

Variations and Fugue " Under the Spreading Chestnut Tree ". *Weinberger*
(Composed for John Barbirolli and the New York Philharmonic Orchestra)
(first time in Manchester)

JOHN BARBIROLLI

Solo Violin : **LAURANCE TURNER**

Solo Flutes : **ARLISS MARRIOTT ; OLIVER BANNISTER**

TICKETS 7/6, 5/-, 3/6, 2/6, 1/6
from Theatre Box Office, Forsyth Bros. Ltd., Deansgate
and Lewis's, Market Street.

CHAS. SEWELL, LTD., PRINTERS, MANCHESTER.

the audience experienced the delights of an almost magical weaving of melodies. For this work a small group of players had been chosen with Mr Laurance Turner in the solo violin part and Mr Arliss Marriott and Mr Oliver Bannister taking the obligati for flutes. The rich and continuous patterning of these leading parts against the background of strings was admirably managed and the three solo artists were most warmly applauded".

Writing of the same concert given on a Sunday afternoon in the Longford Theatre, Stretford, the Evening News critic concurred that "from the opening bars when the flutes fling their ribbons of pure sounds over the insistent strings, one was conscious of the beautiful limpidity of the playing. . . . In the E minor andante with its beautiful flute melody hovering like a white pennant in the clear sky, and the final, most cunningly constructed fugue, both flautists and violinist maintained a fine balance".

Marriott's last season (1944-45) with the orchestra did not include any more notable solo work except for another L'après-midi performance under Albert Coates at Belle Vue on March 11th, but at the end of the season there was a chance for the two 'new boys' to meet a well respected past member of the flute section when the Hallé Pension Fund Concert was given jointly by the BBC Northern and Hallé Orchestras under Barbirolli at the King's Hall, Belle Vue on April 29th. On that occasion Bill Marriott and Oliver Bannister were joined by Norman Seville, the meeting hailing not only the end of the season but the end of Marriott's tenure as principal. He left for Brighton, teaching and freelance work, leaving his chair open to Oliver Bannister.

Oliver Bannister

OLIVER BANNISTER: 1945-1963

In reforming the orchestra in 1943, Barbirolli found several excellent players among the College students, and Oliver Bannister (b.1926), who had entered the RMCM the previous year without fee because of his outstanding accomplishments, joined the Hallé initially as second flute. He had been a pupil of Joe Lingard at the College (where he won the Hiles Medal), and before that with Henry Wilson (1896-1984), a well known theatre musician who played with the Carl Rosa Opera Company and later the National Opera Company of New Zealand.

On Arliss Marriott's departure in 1945, Oliver Bannister became the youngest principal flautist the Hallé has ever known and already fellow musicians were noting his general consistency and beautiful warm rich sound. For £15 a week Hallé principals were giving 52 concerts in Manchester alone each season. Programmes were wide ranging and Barbirolli's concert performances of extracts from Gounod's Romeo & Juliet, Madam Butterfly, Tristan and Aida, along with some deputising in Mussorgsky's Sorochintsy Fair at the Manchester Opera House in 1942, provided Oliver with some early contacts with the operatic repertoire which was to become an important part of his later career.

For the 1946-47 season the orchestra was increased to 80 players and a larger number of woodwind players appeared as soloists - Pat Ryan (clarinet), Charles Cracknell (bassoon), Oliver Bannister amongst them, whilst Archie Camden returned to be soloist in Mozart's Bassoon Concerto. Oliver's solos came in the form of Bach's Suite in B minor, a work favoured by past principals, given on Jan 15th and 16th 1947 and repeated in Bradford on the 17th. Oliver Bannister, the soloist, was seen by critics as a very agreeable flautist who played charmingly and tripped daintily through the finale to a trim and dapper accompaniment.

The orchestra's qualities at this time were recognised by The Times critic who wrote, "discipline and consistency of style that come from the adequate rehearsal and careful training of this orchestra produce results of clarity, precision and expressiveness not at the moment obtainable in any other orchestra . . .", and after one of the Cheltenham Festival concerts readers were told that "in every respect the Hallé, under its present director (J.B.) can stand comparison with the great continental orchestras".

Within four or five years Barbirolli had managed to bring about a change in attitude towards the orchestra and was determined to pursue international status through travel overseas. In May 1948 the orchestra departed for Austria, visiting Innsbruck, Salzburg, Graz and Vienna where critics praised the Hallé's woodwind, mentioning the discipline and rhythmical precision in particular.

Sharing in the accolade was one WIlliam Barlow (1899-1983), an excellent flute and piccolo player who had joined the orchestra in 1945 when Oliver Bannister was made principal. Born in Oldham, he was apprenticed as an engineer on leaving school but was already playing the flute in his spare time, encouraged greatly by Hallé player Billy Thorn who lived not far away. In 1930 there was a recession in engineering and Barlow decided to turn to the flute. He was accepted to play in the Hastings Orchestra under Julius Harrison, playing second to Vernon Harris. Hastings had a winter season then and Bill stayed until 1939. During the summer seasons he played at Harrogate, Whitby, Bexhill, Llandudno and in the Isle of Man, but the outbreak of war put an end to the seaside jobs for a while and Bill returned to engineering before taking on the job of principal flute with the Scottish Orchestra in 1943.

Whilst in Scotland he had the opportunity of performing solos with the orchestra conducted by Warwick Braithwaite in Glasgow and Edinburgh, and December 1944 was a busy month for him as he performed the Mozart Flute & Harp Concerto with Stanley Hopkins (harp) and Bach's Suite in B minor. According to the Scottish critics,

William Barlow

Left to right: Oliver Bannister, Russel King,
William Barlow and Joe Lingard.
The Hague 1949

Barlow distinguished himself playing Bach with a steady tone and a nice sense of style, taking his part with the full success that one expected from a capable soloist.

On leaving the orchestra in 1955, Bill devoted much of his time to teaching and was particularly pleased to have been able to teach a blind boy the flute. Teaching activities continued until he was 80 years of age.

The 1948-49 season at the Albert Hall, Manchester displayed the abilities of wind players Pat Ryan and Charles Cracknell once again in the first English performance of Richard Strauss's Duet Concertino for clarinet and bassoon. Barbirolli's constant attention to his orchestral players and expansion of the repertoire brought the opportunity for wind players to give the first Hallé performance of Guonod's Petite Symphonie, before embarking on a trip to The Hague in April 1949, at which time it was reported that at Leiden the players enjoyed gastronomic delights not available in post-war Britain.

During the same season there was a change in the flute section when Joe Lingard gave up his place to Russell King, who remained for only two seasons, playing third flute and piccolo. This young Australian introduced the sound of the metal flute to the orchestra, and so it was that in 1948 there started a very long and slow decline of the wooden flute sound in the Hallé Orchestra, but it was to be another 35 years or so before an all metal section was realised.

On leaving the orchestra in 1950, King travelled south to join the London Philharmonic Orchestra as third flute and piccolo player, and a year or two later took up the same position with the BBC Symphony Orchestra, eventually returning to Australia in the early 1960's.

King's introduction of the metal flute to the orchestra was short lived however, as his successor, William Morris (1908-1962) played on a Rudall Carte wooden instrument throughout his career. Born in Blackburn, Manchester, Bill Morris first took up the flute with his uncle, Jack Morris who had played for Nellie Melba amongst others, and although the family was musical there wasn't enough money to send him to the College of Music, so before and again just after the war Bill played in a dance band in his home town. The war years proper were spent working in Philips's electrical component factory, but no doubt he found time to keep playing. He was also a good saxophonist and in the late 1940's he played both flute and saxophone in the Winter Gardens, Blackpool and occasionally with Geraldo's Band whenever it happened to come to Blackpool on tour.

By the time he was in his thirties he had saved enough money to enable him to go to the RMCM where he studied with Joe Lingard for two years, after which he joined the Hallé as principal piccolo. The flute section was enhanced by his large, sweet and flexible tone, whilst Manchester benefited generally through his chamber music performances with the Manchester Wind Ensemble and his activities in teaching at the Northern School of Music, where he nurtured a relaxed style of playing. Although a good and kind teacher, Bill never gave up the learning process himself and during his time with the Hallé took the opportunity to go to Paris to have lessons with Caratgé.

The Hallé was all set to enter the 1950's with a particularly strong flute section, and among unfamiliar works conducted by Barbirolli in the 1949-50 season were to be found Jacques Ibert's Flute Concerto and Walter Piston's The Incredible Flautist. The title of Piston's work accurately sums up any flute player who successfully negotiates the fiendishly difficult aforementioned concerto, and it fell to Oliver Bannister to demonstrate what Hallé flautists could do in two performances of the work given in the Albert Hall on 10th and 11th May 1950. The Daily Telegraph reported that "the first Manchester performance of Ibert's flute concerto with the solo part dexterously played by the orchestra's principal flute, Oliver Bannister, left an impression of brittle brilliance in the quick movements and greater depth in the more tranquil andante". Other critics were full of praise too, mentioning Oliver's "dazzling display of skill" and his brilliant technique.

The following year there were no flute solos in the Hallé Concert series but there were two broadcasts featuring two members of the flute section. On January 4th 1951, the BBC broadcast a Hallé concert conducted by Igor Markevitch in which Oliver Bannister and William Barlow gave the first performance in England of Cimarosa's Concerto for Two Flutes & Orchestra, and two months later, on March 1st, Oliver joined the BBC Northern Orchestra and its conductor Charles Groves, as soloist in a performance of Frank Martin's Ballade for flute, piano and strings. The piano part was taken by Maurice Aitchison, well known to Manchester audiences and the concert was broadcast as one of the BBC's Orchestral Hour programmes on a Thursday afternoon.

The early 1950's were busy and exciting times for all members of the orchestra. Janet Craxton represented woodwind players as soloist in Vaughan William's Oboe Concerto, Arnold Bax and Vaughan Williams attended premieres, the orchestra made its first LP record for EMI and its first appearance on BBC Television. There wasn't much time for relaxation and in June 1953 the orchestra left Manchester for a tour of Rhodesia, giving fourteen concerts in fourteen days before returning home to make their first appearance at the London Proms. Even with such a busy schedule there was time for chamber music at the City Art Gallery on Monday evenings for some of the players. Laurance Turner (Hallé leader) had organised a quartet with other Hallé players Hugh Bradley, Sydney Errington and Paul Ward, their numbers being increased by wind and brass players as and when required. Oliver Bannister took part in Roussel's Serenade, and on May 1st 1950 there was Ravel's Introduction & Allegro with Rosemary St. John (harp) and Pat Ryan (clarinet). Other repertoire requiring Oliver's presence included the Beethoven Serenade in D Op.25 given on Jan. 26th 1953.

Repertoire continued to expand in the 1955-56 season with the first performance of Vaughan Williams's eighth symphony on 2nd May 1956, and a new face appeared in the flute section replacing William Barlow. The newcomer was John Braddock whose musical education

Left to right: William Morris, John Braddock and Oliver Bannister

began whilst still a schoolboy in Wiltshire, and on joining the army in 1947 he became a member of the Queen's Own Royal West Surrey Band. Before 1952 he had attended the Kneller Hall Army School of Music, studying with Robert Murchie and then with various players in Germany including Hans Frenz of the Berlin Opera Orchestra, completing his studentship later with John Francis at the Guildhall School of Music 1953-55.

John spent five years with the Hallé as second flute before moving on to the Bournemouth Symphony Orchestra in 1960 where he played piccolo until 1983. A return to the army as Professor of Flute at the Royal Marines School of Music 1983-1990 completed his professional career.

The late 1950's continued with exhausting concert schedules, and as a finale to the centenary celebrations Barbirolli took the orchestra on a tour of Europe in May and June 1958, giving the first concert at Hagen, birthplace of Sir Charles Hallé. Pye recorded the orchestra between 1956 and 1961 and these old LP records now serve to remind us of the orchestra's unmistakable character, and the individuals that formed it during that period. It has been said that during the 1950's Oliver Bannister shaped the whole of the woodwind section, and former leader Martin Milner has written that "Oliver Bannister was so good and of such quality that the other woodwind all played to him. He used to just sit there and turn it out; intonation, phrasing, everything. They automatically played to Oliver and the wind were very, very good because they had this wonderful first flute". Others who played alongside Oliver recognised him not only as a superb flute player but as a person of many cultural interests. His musicianship and personality is such that it was a constant pleasure to work in his section.

In 1958 Oliver made two final appearances as soloist with the Hallé. The work chosen was the same one in which he had first appeared as soloist in 1947 - Bach's Suite in B minor. On January 24th 1958 he played it at Sheffield, repeating it the following day at Leeds. Both concerts were conducted by Paul Hindemith who complimented the orchestra saying - "I had only been working with them for two minutes when I knew: here are musicians with a background, a strongly rooted cultural tradition". In later years Oliver remembered the composer as being a very clear and precise conductor who was business-like in rehearsal but very pleasant in manner.

The early 1960's saw works by Schoenberg, Webern and Berg (Concerto for piano, violin and 13 wind instruments) being scheduled for the first time in Manchester, and tours abroad continued with the Swiss Press commenting on the Hallé's "wonderful woodwind players" in April 1961; but the following year there was tragic news when William Morris's career was brought to an early and sudden close. Driving home after a concert in the south of England a fatal accident occurred not far from home, and he was mourned in public at the next Hallé concert when the orchestra played Elgar's Nimrod.

The following season was to be the last for Oliver Bannister and on 29th September 1963 Barbirolli repeated the first programme he had conducted in Manchester twenty years earlier. That evening Barbirolli presented the Hallé Society's Gold Medal to four players he had engaged that first season. Oliver Bannister of course was one of the four recipients, but was about to leave for Covent Garden where he was to take up the position of Principal Flute, remaining until his retirement in 1986.

The artistry of the Hallé wind players during Oliver Bannister's tenure as principal flute was recognised by everyone as being of the highest quality. There were excellent orchestral players, chamber musicians and soloists amongst them, and in their daily work they maintained a tradition with unique results. For their successors it was indeed a hard act to follow.

Douglas Townshend

DOUGLAS TOWNSHEND AND PETER LLOYD: 1963-1967

In the 1960's pianists once again dominated the soloist scene with notable appearances of John Ogdon, Vladimir Ashkenazy and George Hadjinikos. However, wind players were represented in the Hallé series by Philip Hill who gave the Mozart Oboe Concerto on Jan 16th 1966 and Evelyn Rothwell (Lady Barbirolli) who played the Bax Oboe Concerto on April 21st 1968. Of particular interest to flautists was a visit to Manchester by the English Chamber Orchestra under the direction of John Pritchard giving two concerts on April 1st and 2nd 1964, both of which included a performance of Bach's Suite in B minor with the distinguished soloist, Richard Adeney. Then in his forties, Adeney was principal flute with the London Philharmonic whilst at the same time playing with the English Chamber Orchestra and the Melos Ensemble. He spent much of his time performing chamber music and broadcasted regularly. Such was his reputation that in 1950 Malcolm Arnold had written a flute concerto for him which almost immediately enjoyed popularity amongst flute players.

Joining the Hallé as second flute in 1960 (replacing John Braddock) Douglas Townshend made his way to the principal's chair three years later when Oliver Bannister left for Covent Garden. Born in pre-War Bristol, Douglas had been taught the flute at school by Mary Alexander who was a pupil of the famous Albert Fransella and belonged to the traditional English school of flute playing. Before joining the Hallé he had been a member of the Sadlers Wells Opera Orchestra where he had met and married piccolo player Elizabeth Peerless but he was no stranger to Manchester as his student days began there with lessons from Geoffrey Gilbert and WIlliam Morris at the Northern School of Music. Later there were lessons with William Bennett and Marcel Moyse too. Starting to freelance with orchestras in the north of England meant that Douglas met orchestral flautists of the highest calibre all of whom encouraged and influenced his progress in early days.

His first Manchester concert as principal was on Oct 2nd 1963 when Suo Gan (Welsh Cradle Song) was given in memory of George Weldon, the Hallé Associate Conductor, who did so much to bring much loved music to a wider audience. During that same season he had the unique experience of performing Fauré's Pelléas et Mélisande Suite and the first symphony of Brahms under the baton of the 88 year old Pierre Monteux. The famous heroic flute solo in the symphony's finale rang out loud and clear throughout the whole of the Free Trade Hall and the packed audience was left in no doubt that the metal flute sound had once again found its way into the Hallé section following the example of Russell King's brief encounter in the late 1940's. Douglas Townshend has used Haynes, Flutemakers Guild and Cooper flutes throughout his career but the Hallé principal's chair had not heard or seen the last of the wooden flute as we shall discover later.

The 1960's were unique in many ways and so it was in the orchestra where women now outnumbered the men in the flute section. Although there had been women in other sections of the orchestra for many years Janet Bannerman (b. 1937) and Elizabeth Peerless had the distinction of being the first women flute players in the orchestra's long history. Not only that but they both played metal flutes too, so almost overnight the Hallé had an all metal section which seemed to blend perfectly giving a bright sound to the woodwind and critics were once again mentioning their precision and accuracy.

A Cooper flute, which was popular among flautists then (and still is today) was the chosen instrument of Janet Bannerman who joined the orchestra in 1963, when in her mid-twenties, playing second and alto. She had studied with Derek Honner at the Royal Academy of Music before spending a final two years of study with Caratgé in Paris. By 1966 she had married and the following year left the orchestra to bring up a family. It wasn't until 1973 when she took up the position of second flute with the BBC Northern Symphony Orchestra that she returned to professional flute playing. However, there were performances of chamber music with the Aquilo Wind Quintet and the Hayfield Ensemble to add variety to life as an orchestral musician.

Manchester concerts in the 1960's brought opportunities of meeting and hearing a number of different flute players and orchestras to the student and concert-goer. The London Symphony Orchestra visited the city in April 1964 under its conductor Lorin Maazel and on May 7th of that same year the Bavarian Radio Symphony Orchestra directed by Rafael Kubelik appeared with its distinguished flautist members, Karl Bobzien, Bernhard Walter, Fritz Kirschner, Hans-Dieter Sonntag and Kurt Redel who is now more familiar to us through his recordings. The generally harsher sound and more piercing upper register of this section was to be compared with the warmer, more integrated sound produced by Alan Lockwood, Paul Kingsley and Jack Maine of the Scottish National Orchestra playing in the same hall four months later and the following year comparisons were made when the Warsaw Concert Orchestra under its conductor Stefan Rachon made its first visit to England, playing at the Free Trade Hall, Manchester on 3rd March. Their flute section, made up of three very competent players, produced a similar sound to the Bavarian orchestra but operated more like a trio of soloists than a well moulded section. However, that could not be said of the BBC Symphony Orchestra visiting the same hall on April 8th with a dazzling performance of Bartok's Concerto for Orchestra directed by Antal Dorati. Lead by the incomparable Douglas Whittaker, the BBC flutes blended perfectly into a well rounded section which blended well with the rest of the orchestra. Other members of the flute section on that occasion included David Butt, Clifford Seville (son of past Hallé player Norman Seville) and the excellent piccolo player, Robin Chapman.

During this period the Hallé repertoire was interesting and varied with a proportion of new music being played alongside established masterpieces. Thomas Pitfield, Alan Rawsthorne, Humphrey Searle,

John McCabe and Malcolm Williamson, who was later to become Master of the Queen's Music, provided the new music whilst memorable performances of Mahler's Resurrection Symphony (May 1964), Verdi's Requiem (May 1965), Puccini's Madama Butterfly (concert performances, May 1966), Elgar's Dream of Gereontius and Mahler's Symphony No. 3 (both May 1967), all brought seasons to a close. These seasons brought the usual chances for the principal flute to excel in the form of Daphnis and Chloé (April & Nov. 1964) L'aprés-midi (Oct 1964) and other flute delights which included Beethoven's Rondino for wind instruments on May 3rd 1964. There were tours to Switzerland and Italy in April 1965 and Germany in November 1966. Although these were successful, critics bemoaned the fact that Hallé strings were not sufficient in number and so started an unsettled period in the orchestra's history. Even so, other orchestras visited and large projects were planned. The Royal Liverpool Philharmonic Orchestra gave a concert in the Hallé series on Feb 6th 1966 with the inexhaustible Atarah Ben-Tovim heading flautist colleagues Judy Fenton and John Murphy and later in the same month the BBC Northern Orchestra and the Hallé combined in a performance of Schoenberg's Gurrelieder conducted by George Hurst with Peter Lloyd, Douglas Townshend, Janet Bannerman, David Evans, Roger Rostron (later to become Hallé principal) and Fritz Spiegl performing on flutes and Elizabeth Peerless and Cecil Cox, who later became principal of the BBC orchestra, on piccolos. In spite of all this grand planning and a long list of illustrious soloists audiences began to join the critics in bemoaning the lack of string players and attendances began to fall. Unsettled periods such as these inevitably lead to changes in personnel and it wasn't long before the three flautists were thinking of moving on.

By April 1967 Douglas Townshend and Elizabeth Peerless were leaving for Wales where Douglas was to be principal of the BBC Welsh Orchestra for many years to come and he was later to be heard in broadcasts from Wales but by far the most interesting were those in which he performed as soloist. In 1970 there was a superb performance of Prokofiev's Sonata in D Op. 94 with Harold Lester at the piano and the following year he took the solo part in Visions for flute, piano and strings by Oedeon Partos performed by members of the BBC Welsh Orchestra under Uri Segal. These broadcasts demonstrated his undoubted technical skill and musicianship.

The Hallé management now had the difficult problem of finding three new flute players to take the orchestra to the end of its Manchester season. Francis Nolan was appointed piccolo player and Peter Lloyd as principal with David Evans taking on the job of second flute as freelance player. The orchestra was fortunate in finding three such players at short notice and they performed together as a successful section of the orchestra from April to September 1967.

Although principal for only six months, Peter Lloyd (b.1931) brought not only a beautiful, supple sound to the orchestra but also much experience too, for he had already played second flute with the Scottish National Orchestra for two seasons before coming to Manchester in 1956 to take up the position of principal with the BBC Northern Symphony Orchestra remaining until 1959 when he then returned to the Scottish National Orchestra as principal. Another stint as principal of the BBC Northern Orchestra (1961-66) followed and during all of these years there was much work as a soloist and chamber music player too.

He had been a pupil of the much renowned Edward Walker at the Royal College of Music and later furthered his studies with Fernand Caratgé, Rampal and Moyse in Paris working on development of sound quality. The fruits of his efforts to acquire a beautiful sound are available for all to hear in his recital of French music recorded for 'Pickwick' in Henry Wood Hall, London in May 1989. Here the sound matches the repertoire perfectly in every mood and colour demonstrating his technical assurance and flexible approach to playing the flute.

Since 1974 his chosen instrument has been a Louis Lot flute but during

Peter Lloyd   © Suzie E. Maeder

his Hallé years Cooper and Haynes flutes were favoured delivering some memorable performances in 1967. Barbirolli's performances of Elgar's Gerontius and Mahler's third symphony (May 10/11 1967) in which woodwind and strings excelled themselves stand out in the memory and one can well understand why Peter Lloyd is still to this day saddened by the fact that he had only such a short period under Barbirolli's direction.

Nowadays Peter Lloyd needs no introduction to musical audiences as he is well known as both teacher and performer in this country and abroad. On leaving the Hallé in 1967 he took up the appointment of principal flute with the London Symphony Orchestra staying with them until 1987 when his interest in teaching took him to the U.S.A. and a position of Head of Flute Studies at Indiana University, Bloomington. He also taught flute at the Guildhall School of Music from 1987-93 and continued to appear with the Barry Tuckwell Wind Quintet - an occupation which started during his years with the L.S.O. In 1993 he made his way back to Manchester and is now Head of Flute Studies at the Royal Northern College of Music where students benefit from his vast and varied experience.

Playing second flute during Peter Lloyd's short tenure as Hallé principal was David Evans (b.1941) who had already freelanced occasionally playing second to Douglas Townshend. Before student days David started flute playing on a Rudall Carte wooden instrument but on becoming a pupil of Peter Lloyd at the Royal Manchester College of Music changed to a Louis Lot flute (untuned) which he continued to use when deputising in the Hallé and throughout his short time as second flute there. He later changed to a metal Rudall Carte instrument on which he has played for most of his career.

In 1967 the flute section saw other players sitting in for odd weeks and David never actually signed a contract but continued to play freelance under Lloyd. As David was looking for a more permanent arrangement and relations with the orchestral manager were not altogether amicable

David Evans

he decided to leave the orchestra in September 1967 playing at Stratford for three months followed by a year of freelancing with London orchestras before finally taking up a permanent position with the Iceland Symphony Orchestra.

His final move in 1971 took him to Brazil where he played in the symphony orchestra in Rio. Conditions were very different and he was fortunate in only having to play one week on and one week off in his permanent position there which lasted until 1989 at which time he returned home to England. Whilst in Brazil David filled in his time playing with chamber groups, the Radio Orchestra and the Opera Orchestra. In the 1970's playing Baroque music for weddings in Rio was very lucrative and popular and with all the extra work David was almost able to match his permanent salary paid by the orchestra.

Having seen the Hallé through to the end of a difficult season (1966-67), Peter Lloyd and David Evans prepared themselves for travel as their time with the orchestra was coming to an end and the orchestra went on to spend a few days at the Bordeaux Festival before returning home for its customary visit to the London Proms. Preparation for Barbirolli's Jubilee season which followed in September 1967 was left in the hands of Francis Nolan and two new players in the flute section.

The Jubilee season opened with Richard Strauss's magnificent tone poem Ein Heldenleben and proved to be one of the most memorable in Hallé history having fifty concerts in Manchester alone and twenty two new works added to the repertoire. Although the orchestra was highly praised for its performances the flute section remained in disarray and with Peter Lloyd and David Evans disappearing from the scene, the Hallé management still had not been able to find flute players to replace them on permanent contract and so the season saw freelance players come and go for a while. The first concerts of the season were taken on by Christopher Taylor (1929-1983) and Fritz Spiegl (b.1926) with the young Francis Nolan (b.1949) playing piccolo.

Chris Taylor was well known as a good freelance player and it was his versatility and adaptability which made him in much demand throughout his career. He was a product of Geoffrey Gilbert's teaching accepting the French style of flute playing which was so new to British players earlier this century. Through its use, and later his appointment as professor at the Royal Academy he furthered the cause for its acceptance among British players. His numerous recordings are an example of his artistry and demonstrate his excellent intonation, good phrasing and individual sound. He was interested in everything musical including flute design and played a part in developing Albert Cooper's instruments - particularly his alto and bass flutes. Before his Manchester days, Chris was principal flute in the Royal Opera House Orchestra and later, the Royal Philharmonic. Sadly, he died all too soon, on September 30th 1982, a victim of Leukaemia but all through his final days he continued to work with dedication offering much inspiration to others.

Chris Taylor's freelance partner in 1967 was Fritz Spiegl, now well known to us as not only a musician but a writer and broadcaster too. He was born in Austria but grew up with a family in England where music was encouraged. There were lessons with Richard Adeney as a boy but at 16 he took a job as an office boy and studied art in the evenings. (His cartoon drawings adorn many Liverpool Philharmonic flute parts and amuse flautists at rehearsals to this day). In the 1940's he bought his first flute - a Rudall Carte ebonite instrument - and joined amateur orchestras in and around London but by 1947 he was entering the Royal Academy of Music and began lessons with Gareth Morris. One year later he was offered the position of principal flute with the Royal Liverpool Philharmonic staying until 1963.

Staying in Liverpool Fritz later found time to start writing and broadcasting as well as forming the Liverpool Wind Ensemble with other members of the orchestra there but when he left the Liverpool Philharmonic Orchestra in 1963 Sir Malcolm Sargent asked him to do a tour of America with the Royal Philharmonic as principal flute and this was the beginning of life as a freelance player. It was indeed fortunate that the Hallé was able to call upon the services of high calibre freelance players such as Chris Taylor and Fritz Spiegl in difficult times.

Roger Rostron

ROGER ROSTRON: 1967 ONWARDS

The arrival of Roger Rostron in November 1967 brought the return of the wooden flute to the Hallé. One of his instruments originally belonged to Gerald Jackson (b.1900), a principal with the Royal Philharmonic under Sir Thomas Beecham and Roger once described its rare quality as being "comparable to a Strad". He used this same instrument for almost twenty years before finally abandoning it to a gold Powell with Trevor James headjoint in the mid-eighties.

Born in Leicester in 1937, Roger moved to Torquay at the age of nine where he later attended the Grammar School. There he studied music with J. Burman Hopwood with whom he was to give a recital many years later at Paignton Parish Church, Torbay (29th July 1971) to much acclaim. The critic of the Herald Express wrote, "that Mr Rostron is a master of his craft was never in doubt for a moment and he was admirably supported by Mr Hopwood". He went on to say that, "In Debussy's Syrinx for unaccompanied flute and Faure's Fantasie for Flute & Piano, Rostron secured a brilliant but never cutting tone in the instrument's higher reaches, and a beautiful mellowness of tone in its lower register".

At school Roger's first instrument was a fife but his first strict flute lessons were with James Long, a theatre musician of Torquay. He later travelled to Dartington Hall for further lessons before serious flute studies began with John Francis (b. 1908) at the age of 17 and continued on entering the Royal College of Music where he later studied with Edward Walker (1909-1982).

National Service (1956-59) followed and he spent his time with the Band of the Irish Guards where he helped provide the famous marching tune and whistling for the film Bridge on the River Kwai. He toured Canada, the United States, Honolulu and Australia with the band and gained much experience which was to benefit his career after demobilisation. On leaving the army he spent nearly three years as second flute with Sadler's Wells Opera Orchestra before he moved North to Manchester in 1962 to become sub-principal flute with the BBC Northern Symphony Orchestra and remained there until his appointment of principal flute with the Hallé Orchestra. From that time onwards listeners have admired his fluent and accurate playing in pieces such as Debussy's L'après midi-d'un faune and Ravel's Daphnis & Chloé amongst others.

His first season with the orchestra (1967-68) proved to be a particularly busy time during which twenty two new works were added to the repertoire and he found himself hurled headlong into Messaien's Turangalila Symphony, Lutoslawski's Concerto for Orchestra and a complete performance of Berlioz's Trojans before setting off on a forty two day tour of South America at the end of the season. This tour included twenty three concerts in eight different countries and meant that by the age of thirty Roger Rostron had played the flute on every continent of the world. The press reported that the orchestra at this time was "impeccable and superb".

Roger's colleagues in this mammoth undertaking were Raymond Hill Fritz Spiegl and Francis Nolan. Raymond Hill joined the orchestra as second flute in 1968 remaining for the next fourteen years before leaving for New South Wales where he married and settled, putting his time and energy into teaching. Fritz Spiegl was not on permanent contract at this time and John Barrow had been brought in at the beginning of the 1967-68 season for a performance of Strauss's Ein Heldenleben but departed in 1969 leaving the flute section down to three in number for the next ten years. John is still to be heard playing in and around Manchester as principal flute with the Manchester Camerata Orchestra.

The piccolo player, Francis Nolan had been a member of the orchestra for longer than Roger's other two colleagues having replaced Elizabeth Peerless in April 1967 and his appointment as principal piccolo was the

Francis Nolan

first major appointment of his career. Born in Liverpool in 1949, Francis Nolan became a pupil of Atarah Ben-Tovim and Geoffrey Gilbert at the Royal Manchester College of Music, and remaining with the Hallé for nearly three years he distinguished himself as one of the best and most reliable piccolo players to emerge from the RMCM for some time and indeed his subsequent career reflects this. On leaving the Hallé in 1970 he moved to the BBC Symphony Orchestra and also played with the Academy of St. Martin. Since 1973 he has played as principal piccolo with that venerable institution, the London Symphony Orchestra and is also Professor of Piccolo at the Guildhall School of Music & Drama, London. Although he plays on a Brannen Cooper silver flute, he prefers to use all-wooden piccolos made by Powell and Seaman. The sound he produces in the highest register of his instrument verges on the sweet rather than the shrill, although like all piccolo players, he can manage the latter quite well when the necessity arises. His ability to play 'pianissimo' in the high register without loss of tone quality has gained him much respect and puts him head and shoulders above the average.

For any wind player listening to Hallé concerts in the 1968-69 season there were a few highlights which remain in the memory. In a performance of L'Enfance du Christ the flute section distinguished itself in exhibiting a beautiful sound of liquid quality in the famous trio for two flutes and harp, and later the whole of the wind section got a chance to shine in a performance of Strawinsky's Concerto for piano and wind conducted by Laurance Foster on December 8th 1968. After the Christmas break Roger Rostron was heard to good effect once again in Debussy's L'après-midi d'un faune conducted by Moshe Atzmon on 26th January 1969 and his playing of this famous solo on his wooden flute had an ethereal quality about it, floating on a warm sea of sound provided by the rest of the orchestra complementing the soloist's exquisite performance. In the words of the Telegraph critic, "Roger Rostron's flute playing in particular had the right suggestion of hazy tranquillity".

We didn't have to wait long after that before the new principal was appearing as soloist in Bach's Brandenburg Concerto No.5 in D with Martin Milner (violin) and Alan Cuckston (harpsichord). Following the tradition of past principals Roger Rostron took on the demanding flute part of this work on Thursday February 13th 1969, and the performance was enjoyed by many but received an unfavourable review from the Guardian critic, Gerald Larner who considered it dull and unexciting. At this time critics were not really interested in performances of Baroque music of any kind at Hallé concerts as they used to complain about the size of ensembles used and the size of the hall etc., all of which they thought inappropriate for the music.

At the beginning of the following season Roger Rostron appeared once again as soloist along with Jean Bell in two performances of Mozart's Flute & Harp Concerto conducted by Maurice Handford at the Hallé's Industrial Concerts series in the Free Trade Hall on 29/30th October 1969. On these occasions there was nothing to complain about and the Manchester Evening News critic, John Robert Blunn wrote in the form of an amusing letter from one industrial worker to another saying, "Dear Fred . . . The Hallé flute chap, Roger Rostron and the orchestra's No.1 harpist played well in that Mozart thing for flute and harp." Praise for Roger's performances within the orchestra continued throughout the season, the culmination of which came in the Daily Telegraph on 27th April 1970 when Michael Kennedy exclaimed that 'in Debussy's L'après-midi d'un faune the flute playing of Roger Rostron and Philip Hill's solos were beyond praise".

In the same season Roger took part in a very bright and happy performance of Bach's Brandenburg Concerto No.2 with Philip Hill (oboe), Martin Milner (violin) and Maurice Murphy (trumpet) on February 1st 1970. This performance conducted by Maurice Handford was hailed in the Guardian the next day as "the most respectable performance of a Brandenburg Concerto in Hallé history(!)".

Barbirolli's programmes for the same season included a performance of Delius's Appalachia offering the flautists a rare chance to perform altogether on piccolos and the concert prompted Gerald Larner of the Guardian to observe not only the high quality of the orchestra's performance but 'the emergence of Roger Rostron as one of the very best orchestral flautists in this country".

At the end of the season the orchestra suffered a great loss when Francis Nolan departed for London leaving Roger Rostron and Raymond Hill to start the 1970-71 season with replacement piccolo player, Andrew Cunningham. Apart from his busy concert schedule Roger still found time to teach at the RNCM, write reviews of new music for 'Music Teacher' magazine and to perform in chamber music recitals with the Hallé Wind Quintet throughout the 1970's and on into the next decade, and as a consequence of assisting the L.S.O. as Co-principal Flute during their tour of Rumania, Czechoslovakia and Hungary in 1968/69, he was also invited to appear as guest principal with that same orchestra for their International Series of concerts, 1970-71.

The Hallé Wind Quintet made its Manchester debut at the RNCM on 31st March 1973 and Roger Rostron along with other Hallé players Barry Davis (oboe), James Gregson (clarinet), Robert Blackburn (horn) and Martin Hardy (bassoon) presented a well balanced programme of music by Danzi, Beethoven, Arnold and Carter, also including the premiere of Manino's Mini Quartet Op.74. The concert was brought to a close with a performance of Poulenc's Sextet with Rayson Whalley at the piano. Other engagements followed in and around Manchester and the quintet travelled to venues in Yorkshire, the Lake District and Sheffield amongst others. They also made a recording (Lighter Music for Wind Quintet, ALM 602) for Amberlee Records three years after their debut concert.

From 1977 onwards Roger was flute player with the Manchester Baroque Ensemble which comprised of Hallé players and gave concerts in many parts of the north west as well as a series of concerts at St. Ann's Church in Manchester where its reception bore witness to audience interest in music of the seventeenth and eighteenth centuries. The ensemble travelled as far as Belfast to perform where it was welcomed by the critic of the Belfast Telegraph in May 1978. Lighter 'entertainment' music of the baroque period was often featured in their programmes and sometimes the ensemble was augmented by guest singers and instrumentalists. In addition, the harpsichord was replaced by the piano for music of later periods up to and including that of the twentieth century. During this period Roger also gave solo recitals from time to time accompanied by pianists such as Rayson Whalley, Paul Derrett or Stephen Pilkington and after one such event at least one critic noted "the sure touch of a master of the flute" and went on to say that "his mid-day recital at Bolton Central Library was a delight in its precision, assurance and musicality".

The 1970's bought regular praise to the Hallé woodwind players from newspaper critics and Roger Rostron's contributions were singled out. There was the admirably played flute solo in the Pantomime movement of Ravel's Second Suite from Daphnis & Chloé, the agile flute playing in the Scherzo of Mendelssohn's Midsummer Night's Dream, the pure and liquid sound in Ravel's La Flute Enchantée, the eloquent solo in Holst's The Perfect Fool, the exquisite flute solo which began Ravel's Bolero and in the Telegraph on 24th September 1975 Michael Kennedy noted how "Roger Rostron's playing in the adagio (Dvorak's Cello Concerto) matched Tortelier's expressive phrasing".

Although the wind players were at a peak they were also working a 40 hour week. Recordings were made for EMI with Barbirolli's successor, James Loughran and the orchestra managed to attract visiting musicians of the highest calibre. Arvid Yansons brought his own orchestra - the Leningrad Philharmonic - to Manchester on 23rd September 1971 giving concertgoers a chance to hear their flautists, Valentin Cherenkov, Evgeny Matveyev, Stanislav Poschekhov and

Alexandra Vavilina in an excellent performance of Shostakovich's fifth symphony.

The Hallé's own flute section saw change at the end of the 1972-73 season when Andrew Cunningham left for Oslo and Christine Hulme arrived in October 1973 standing in for one season only. The following year Ronald Marlowe (b.1948) filled the vacancy and was appointed principal piccolo and has been an important member of the Hallé flute section ever since. He helped bring some stability to the section and has demonstrated much reliability over the last twenty years or so. This Londoner whose ambition has always been to play in orchestras rather than perform as a chamber musician or soloist, was a pupil of Harold Clarke at Trinity College of Music1968-71, and before his appointment with the Hallé spent the first three years of his career as sub-principal flute with the BBC Welsh Orchestra (1971-74).

However, it is usually the principal who appears as soloist from time to time and Roger Rostron's appearance as such in a performance of Devienne's Flute Concerto No.8 in G on November 11th 1973 pleased all the critics who seemed to agree on the merits of his playing. Gerald Larner of the Guardian, who had been so uncomplimentary about Roger's previous appearance as soloist now commented that he "gave a performance of rare agility and elegance", and after having mentioned his skill and artistry the Telegraph critic concluded - "If Devienne's amiable music is to undergo a process of rejuvenation, it will do so only by means of such quality performances. It was flute playing at its most accomplished". John Robert Blunn of the Manchester Evening News joined in the praise with, "Rostron's solo performance of Devienne's flute concerto No.8 in G was the most delightful part of last night's concert at the Free Trade Hall, providing a happy link between Mozart's 29th symphony and Beethoven's Eroica. It is the sort of neo-baroquery which engages and entertains and Rostron's playing should have made optimists of us all - In the difficult opening allegro Rostron's phrasing was neatly pointed creating lovely pure sounds. In the adagio Rostron's artistry was more obvious and rather more convincing, just as in the last movement there was a confident return to technical display. A very satisfying performance". In the eyes of the critics and the Hallé audience Roger Rostron had proved himself to be a soloist of some stature with this performance of a virtually unknown work.

There were to be more performances of the concerto at the end of the season. Two of these were at out of town concerts, the first being at Preston Guild Hall on June 1st 1974 and the second at Roger's home town of Leicester nearly one week later when the writer in the Leicester Mercury on 8th June 1974 noted that "Rostron brought a beautifully cool tone and made the most intricate embellishments sound like child's play. Loughran made sure the orchestra was properly restrained in volume and achieved perfectly that give and take essential in concertos of the late eighteenth century".

The last of the three performances took place on 5th July 1974 in the Free Trade Hall, Manchester as part of a Hallé Prom Concert and was well received. It had been a triumphant season for Roger but also one during which he had been extremely worried about the loss of a wooden headjoint belonging to his much loved 'Jackson' instrument. After giving the headjoint to another musician to take to Glasgow for repairs, the bag containing the headjoint and an evening suit was stolen at the station there and appeals in the press came to nothing. Only much later was it miraculously found in a dustbin in Glasgow!

The 1970's continued with what seemed to be fairly unimaginative programme planning but other orchestras still visited Manchester providing alternative selections while the Hallé went on tour to Germany and Switzerland (January 1975) as well as making a visit to the Hong Kong Festival in February 1976. Of all the visitors to Manchester, of particular interest to flautists was James Galway's appearance as soloist and director of the Zagreb Soloists in a programme of mainly Bach and a few years later on 21st February 1980 there was a

FREE TRADE HALL, at 7.30 p.m.
SUNDAY, 11th NOVEMBER, 1973

HALLÉ ORCHESTRA

Leaders
Martin Milner   Michael Davis

conductor
JAMES LOUGHRAN

soloist
ROGER ROSTRON

---

programme

National Anthem

MOZART
Symphony No. 29 in A

DEVIENNE
Flute Concerto No. 8

interval

BEETHOVEN
Symphony No. 3 in E flat (Eroica)

memorable performance of Bach's Brandenburg Concert No.5 given by the Leipzig Gewandhaus Bach Orchestra with Heinz Hortzsch as flute soloist.

That same year the Hallé flute section was made up to four player's with the arrival of Jonathan Booty who was appointed Assistant Principal. He first took up the flute at the age of twelve and later studied at the Royal College of Music with Graham Maygar, winning the Eve Kirsch Prize. On leaving the college he continued to study for another year with Michel Dubost in Paris on a French Government Scholarship before returning to Britain in 1980. Since that time he has not only proved to be an extremely valuable asset to the Hallé flute section but has also given solo flute recitals throughout the North West region and played as chamber musician performing with the Free Trade Winds, a quintet whose members have been assistant principal wind players in the orchestra. Of course, Jonathan has been heard on many occasions in the role of principal. On 2nd October 1994 the orchestra gave a performance of Appalachia by Delius and this was a rare occasion indeed for not only did Jonathan Booty take the principal's chair demonstrating a flexible tone and beautiful clear ringing sound in his solos but also displayed his adaptability in making quick changes between flute and piccolo as directed in the Delius score. Appalachia is one of those rare pieces in which the whole flute section play piccolos and Jonathan Booty, Hilary Pooley and Ronald Marlowe made a handsome sound as piccolo trio, blending well with the rest of the orchestra.

At the end of the 1981-82 season Raymond Hill left the orchestra for a better climate and wasn't replaced until February 1983 when John Grant (b.1960) arrived in Manchester having spent the previous year as second flute with the Scottish Ballet. John is a native of Ayreshire and began his musical training with David Nicholson at the Royal Scottish Academy of Music, later completing his studies with David Butt at the Royal College of Music, London. He remained with the Hallé for three

John Grant   © Williamson

years before his appointment as principal with the Scottish Opera Orchestra and a further move one year later took him to the principal's chair in the Royal Scottish Orchestra with whom he has subsequently appeared as soloist. Other activities in recent years have included appearances as chamber musician with the Scottish Wind Quintet and the Allauder Ensemble.

During the early 1980's James Galway made several visits to Manchester giving Mancunians a chance to assess and enjoy his musicianship. On his first visit (17th July 1983) he directed and performed both Mozart concertos in the same programme at the Palace Theatre but on 29th November 1983 he returned with the Ulster Orchestra who paid tribute to Hamilton Harty with a performance of his "With the Wild Geese". Bryden Thompson conducted whilst Galway was soloist in Mozart's Concert in G. The Manchester Evening News critic wrote the following day that "Galway demonstrated not only his remarkable vibrato and breath demanding virtuosity but also fine musicianship in the Mozart". The following year (23rd November 1984) almost to the day, Galway returned with more Mozart performances - the Concerto in D and the Concerto for Flute & Harp with Marisa Robles - but on January 7th of that same year he had appeared with the Chamber Orchestra of Europe giving both Mozart concertos in the same evening and prompted one critic to write, "Galway was positively brilliant", but some concertgoers expressed disappointment at the choice of repertoire.

The Hallé's own concerts in the early 1980's brought performances by several members of the orchestra as soloists including of course Roger Rostron but for him there was also a new departure as conductor. On November 29th 1983 he conducted the orchestra's wind, brass and percussion sections on platform 10 at Manchester's Piccadilly Station at the naming ceremony of a British Rail locomotive. Appropriately enough it was named 'Sir Charles Hallé'. Occasional appearances as conductor continued on into the 1990's for the benefit of Hallé appeals and sponsorship.

By 1986 John Grant was departing for Scotland where he too would get his chances of solo appearances. He was not replaced for the 1986-87 season and this left the flute section down to three in number until the following season when Hilary Jones joined the orchestra as second flute continuing after 1989 under her married name, Hilary Pooley.

However, Roger Rostron made his only solo appearance of the decade in Bach's Brandenburg Concerto No.5 in D on February 28th 1985 with Pan Hon Lee (violin) and Janet Simpson whose harpsichord playing was singled out for special mention by one critic who also thought "the playing generally was lively and rhythmically alert, particularly in the jolly finale".

With the arrival of the 1990's came another visit from the London Symphony Orchestra (23rd Sept. 1990) with a performance of a new flute concerto by John McCabe. Michael Tilson Thomas directed the orchestra and the dedicatee, James Galway, was the admirable soloist who was also required to play the alto flute on this occasion. The three orchestral flutes played by Paul Edmund-Davies (principal), Martin Parry and Francis Nolan were placed not together, as is customary, but spread out in the orchestra from left to right across the platform. The reason for this was soon apparent as their parts echoed the soloist's phrases in the first section of this continuous composition. Francis Nolan was back on home ground so to speak and in characteristically reliable style matched Galway's playing perfectly in the echo sequences.

The appearance of members of the Hallé Orchestra as soloists has continued in recent years and Roger Rostron has taken on his fair share of work in this respect maintaining a proud tradition. In 1991 he was involved with other members of the orchestra in presenting Moschele's Concerto for Flute & Oboe and Bach's Brandenburg Concerto No.4 in G. Roger was joined by principal oboe, Richard Simpson in no fewer than three performances of the Moscheles concerto in February 1991 to much acclaim and the Manchester Evening News critic, Robert Beale, spoke for the whole audience in writing, "Their performance was a fine

Left to right: Ron Marlowe, Hilary Pooley,
Roger Rostron, Jonathan Booty.

© Ruth Treloar

testimonial to the skill of Hallé's players".

Five months later (July 1991) Roger and assistant principal, Jonathan Booty came together in a performance of Bach's fourth Brandenburg Concerto, conducted by Michael Davis, in which they proved to be a very well matched pair prompting one critic to write that "this stimulating baroque evening was an exciting showcase for the Hallé's own talented soloists". Of the performance, the same critic went on to write - "First we were enchanted by the exquisite flautistry of Roger Rostron and Jonathan Booty in the fourth Brandenburg Concerto, complemented by the artistry of Michael David's violin. The echo effects were hauntingly beautiful and Janet Simpson's harpsichord added richly to the texture". It is interesting to note that the critics were no longer writing quibbling notices about the pros and cons of Baroque performance as they had been doing some years earlier, but instead, were ready to point out the skill and talent of the Hallé players.

In the last decade of the century Manchester's music remains interesting and varied through the efforts of professional, amateur and student musicians and it is the Hallé Orchestra who, in one way or another, encourages those who choose to visit the city too. The St. Petersburg Philharmonic under the direction of Mariss Yansons closed the Hallé season on 20th May 1993 with an excellent account of Shostakovich's Leningrad Symphony in which the principal flute, Valentin Zverev played his solos with a firmly centred tone and well controlled vibrato. Also to be heard were passages of perfectly matched triple tonguing from the whole flute section and piccolo player, Evgeny Matveev produced a firm straight sound of excellent timbre throughout the whole range of his instrument. In the finale, the flutes stood out above the whole orchestra exhibiting excellent ensemble, attack and intonation. Rarely does a flute section manage to pierce the dense orchestral texture of the finale climaxes as this one did and without the existence of the Hallé Orchestra rarely would Manchester audiences get the chance to experience different performance practices.

The opening of Manchester's G-Mex Centre has brought one or two large scale concerts attracting international artists such as Jose Carreras (Dec.1991) and Kiri Te Kanawa (Nov. 1992) but there was one event at the same venue which caused comparisons to be made with Manchester music makers of earlier times. The concert alluded to here went under the title of "Classical Spectacular" and featured popular repertoire performed by the Hallé Orchestra with tenor and baritone soloists, chorus, Band of the Scots Guards, Band of the Irish Guards, muskets, cannons and lasers! All this served as a reminder of Edward de Jong's monster concerts of the 1870's. If laser lighting had been available to him, Mr de Jong would have loved it!

From its humble beginnings and its founder's ideas the Hallé Orchestra has attained international recognition and continues to attract orchestral players and soloists of the highest calibre due to the efforts and artistry of the musicians mentioned in these pages and to their colleagues of yesterday and today.

APPENDIX 1

Flute Players - Hallé Orchestra 1858 - 1993

1858-59   Edward De Jong
                Mr Berry

1859-70   Edward De Jong
                R. Charlton

1871-72   F. Brossa
                O. Gaggs

1872-75   F. Brossa
                H. Piddock

1876-77   F. Brossa
                H. Piddock
                F. Lax (picc)

1877-85   F. Brossa
                H. Piddock
                V. L. Needham (picc)

1885-88   F. Brossa
                H. Piddock
                L. F. Strelitskie (picc)

1888-99   F. Brossa
                H. Piddock
                V. L. Needham (picc)

1899-1900 F. Brossa
                V. L. Needham
                T. B. Marsden
                W. Dixon

1900-04	V. L. Needham
	E. S. Redfern
	T. B. Marsden *(F. Hatton replaced Marsden, Feb. 1904)*
	W. Dixon
1904-13	V. L. Needham
	E. S. Redfern
	W. Dixon
	F. Hatton
1913-14	V. L. Needham
	E. S. Redfern
	F. Hatton
1914-16	V. L. Needham
	E. S. Redfern
	J. Lingard
1916-17	E. S. Redfern *(A. Halstead, first concert of season only)*
	J. Lingard
	W. Thorn
1917-21	E. S. Redfern
	J. Lingard
	W. Thorn
1921-25	J. Lingard
	J. Ridgway
	W. Thorn (picc)
1925-26	J. Lingard
	J. Ridgway
	W. Thorn (picc)
	N. Seville

1926-28	J. Lingard
	W. Thorn (picc)
	N. Seville
	K. Whittaker
1928-30	J. Lingard
	W. Thorn (picc)
	N. Seville
	J. Ridgway
1930-33	J. Lingard
	W. Thorn (picc)
	N. Seville
	G. Gilbert
1933-34	J. Lingard
	W. Thorn
	N. Seville
1934-35	Geoffrey Gilbert
	W. Thorn (picc)
	N. Seville
1935-37	Vernon Harris
	W. Thorn (picc)
	N. Seville
1937-43	Vernon Harris
	N. Seville (picc)
	J. Lingard
1943-45	Arliss Marriott
	Oliver Bannister
	Joseph Lingard

1945-48	Oliver Bannister
	William Barlow (picc)
	Joseph Lingard
1948-50	Oliver Bannister
	William Barlow
	Russell King (picc)
1950-55	Oliver Bannister
	William Barlow
	William Morris (picc)
1955-60	Oliver Bannister
	John Braddock
	William Morris (picc)
1960-62	Oliver Bannister
	Douglas Townshend
	William Morris (picc)
1962-63	Oliver Bannister
	Douglas Townshend
	Elizabeth Peerless (picc)
1963-67	Douglas Townshend
	Janet Bannerman
	Elizabeth Peerless (picc)
Apr-Sept 1967	Peter Lloyd
	David Evans
	Francis Nolan
1967-68	Christopher Taylor
	Fritz Spiegl
	Francis Nolan (picc)

1968-69	Roger Rostron
	Raymond Hill
	Francis Nolan (picc)
	John Barrow

1968-69 Roger Rostron
Raymond Hill
Francis Nolan (picc)
John Barrow

1969-70 Roger Rostron
Raymond Hill
Francis Nolan

1970-73 Roger Rostron
Raymond Hill
Andrew Cunningham (picc)

1973-74 Roger Rostron
Raymond Hill
Christine Hulme (picc)

1974-79 Roger Rostron
Raymond Hill
Ronald Marlowe (picc)

1979-80 Roger Rostron
Raymond Hill
Ronald Marlowe (picc)
(Jonathan Booty appointed assistant principal, 1980)

1980-82 Roger Rostron
Raymond Hill
Ronald Marlowe (picc)
Jonathan Booty

1982-86 Roger Rostron
Jonathan Booty
John Grant *(appointed second flute, 1983)*
Ronald Marlowe (picc)

1986-87	Roger Rostron
	Jonathan Booty
	Ronald Marlowe (picc)
1987-89	Roger Rostron
	Hilary Jones
	Jonathan Booty
	Ronald Marlowe (picc)
1989-	Roger Rostron
	Hilary Pooley
	Jonathan Booty
	Ronald Marlowe (picc)

APPENDIX 2

TEACHER PUPIL RELATIONSHIP IN HALLÉ FLAUTISTS

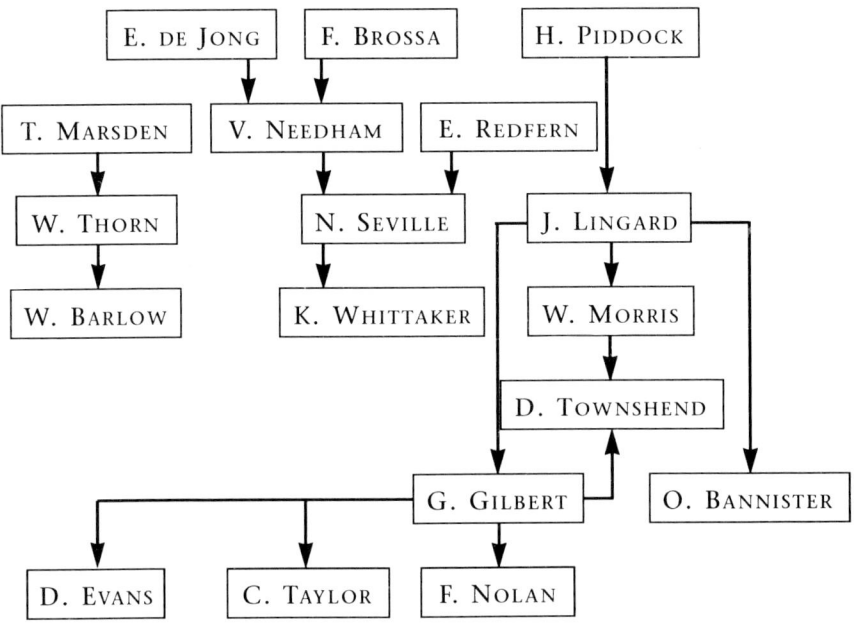

Pupil - teacher relationships in Hallé flautists span more than 100 years and the tradition thus established is unique to British orchestras.

Appendix 3

List of Solos Played by Hallé Flautists 1858-93

Unless stated otherwise all solos listed were given in the Free Trade Hall, Manchester, at Hallé Concerts.

EDWARD DE JONG

29th Sept. 1858	Boehm, Fantasia on Scottish Airs
10th Nov. 1858	Verdi, Grand Selection from Il Travatore
17th Nov. 1858	Boehm, Fantasia on Beethoven's "Le Desir"
5th Jan. 1859	Boehm, Fantasia on German Airs
16th Mar. 1859	Boehm, Fantasia on Swiss Airs
7th Dec. 1859	Furstenau, Fantasia on Norma
29th Feb. 1860	Richardson, There's nae luck
18th Apr. 1860	Boehm, Fantasia on 'Swiss Boy'
9th Jan. 1862	Briccialdi, Airs from Lucrezia Borgia
26th Nov. 1863	Paggi, Fantasie on Neopolitan Airs
11th Feb. 1864	E. de Jong, Scotch Airs
4th Dec. 1864	E. de Jong, Fantasia on Faust
12th Jan. 1865	Demersseman, Grand Duet (with Lavigne, oboe)
16th Nov. 1865	E. de Jong, Fantasia on Scotch and Irish Airs
28th Dec. 1865	Demersseman, Grand Duet (with Lavigne, oboe)
8th Feb. 1866	Molique, Andante & Finale from Concerto in D
6th Dec. 1866	Jacoby, Duet on Scotch Airs (with Lavigne, oboe)
31st Jan. 1867	E. de Jong, Fantasia on Faust

JEAN FIRMIN BROSSA

14th Dec. 1871	Demersseman, Fantasia on a melody by Chopin
4th Jan. 1872	Hummel, Septet in D min.

	(Hallé and section principals)
18th Jan. 1872	Demersseman, Fantasia in G, Il Tremelo
19th Jan. 1899	Bach, Suite No.2 in B min

VINCENT NEEDHAM

31st Oct. 1901	Handel, Sweet Bird (Il Penseroso), Lilian Blauvelt (sop)
1st Dec. 1904	Bach, Brandenburg Concerto No.4 (with E. S. Redfern)
15th Nov. 1906	Bach, Suite No.2 in B min
7th Jan.1909	Bach, Suite No.2 in B min
18th Feb. 1909	Bach, Brandenburg Concerto No.5
18th Mar. 1909	Bach, Suite No.2 in B min
4th Dec. 1913	Bach, Brandenburg Concerto No.4 (with E. S. Redfern)

JOSEPH LINGARD

10th Nov. 1921	Bishop, Lo here the gentle lark (with Agnes Nichols)
1st Feb. 1923	Bach, Suite No.2 in B min
25th Oct. 1923	Mozart, Flute & Harp Concerto (with Charles Collier)
5th Mar. 1925	Bach, Suite No.2 in B min
19th Mar. 1925	Godard, Suite for flute & orch.
7th Jan. 1926	Holst, Fugal Concerto (with A. Whittaker, oboe)
28th Oct. 1926	Bach, Brandenburg Concerto No.5

VERNON HARRIS

| 5th Nov. 1936 | Bach, Brandenburg Concerto No.5 |
| 1st Mar. 1942 | Bach, Brandenburg Concerto No.5 |

ARLISS MARRIOTT

16th Jan. 1944	Bach, Brandenburg Concerto No.4
	(with Oliver Bannister)
	Longford Theatre, Stretford
	(repeated at Sheffield 14/1/44,
	Bradford 15/01/44, Hanley 03/02/44)

OLIVER BANNISTER

15th Jan. 1947	Bach, Suite No.2 in B min
	(Albert Hall, Manchester)
16th Jan. 1947	Bach, Suite No.2 in B min
	(Albert Hall, Manchester)
17th Jan. 1947	Bach, Suite No.2 in B min (at Bradford)
10th May 1950	Ibert, Flute Concerto
	(Albert Hall, Manchester)
11th May 1950	Ibert, Flute Concerto
	(Albert Hall, Manchester)
4th Jan. 1951	Cimarosa, Concerto for Two Flutes & Orch
	(with W. Barlow)
	(Hallé broadcast, BBC Third Programme)
1st Mar. 1951	Martin, Ballade for flute strings & piano
	(Broadcast with BBC Northern/Groves,
	Third Programme)
24th Jan. 1958	Bach, Suite No.2 in B min
	(at Sheffield with Hindemith)
25th Jan. 1958	Bach, Suite No.2 in B min
	(at Leeds with Hindemith)

ROGER ROSTRON

13th Feb. 1969	Bach, Brandenburg Concerto No.5
29th/30th Oct. 1969	Mozart, Concerto in C for Flute & Harp
	(with Jean Bell)
1st Feb. 1970	Bach, Brandenburg Concerto No.2
11th Nov. 1973	Devienne, Flute Concerto No.8

1st June 1974	Devienne, Flute Concerto No.8 (Preston Guild Hall)
7th June 1974	Devienne, Flute Concerto No.8 (Leicester)
5th July 1974	Devienne, Flute Concerto No.8
28th Feb. 1985	Bach, Brandenburg Concerto No.5
13th Feb. 1991	Moscheles Concerto for Flute & Oboe (with Richard Simpson)
14th Feb. 1991	Moscheles Concerto for Flute & Oboe (with Richard Simpson)
17th Feb. 1991	Moscheles Concerto for Flute & Oboe (with Richard Simpson)
2nd July 1991	Bach, Brandenburg Concerto No.4 (with Jonathan Booty)

APPENDIX 4

Early BBC Broadcasts given by Hallé Flautists

10.4.24   **Joseph Lingard**
Molique - Andante from Concerto
Kohler - Papillon
Woodall - Serenade
Paggi - Rimembranza Napoletane

20.4.24   **Manchester Wind Quintet: Joseph Lingard (f1),**
S. Whittaker (ob)
H. Mortimer (cl), O. Paersch (hn), A. C. Camden (bn)
Lefebvre - Quintette Op. 57
Holbrooke - Quintet (Lament & Scherzo)
Grainger - Walking Tune
Purcell - Cebell
Barthe - Aubade
Lully - Minuet
Sobeck - Scherzino
Onslow - Quintet Op.81 in F
Val Hamm - Trio for flute, oboe & clarinet
Pierne - Pastorale
Pessard - Prelude & Minuet
Barthe - Passacaille
Sobeck - Tarantelle

26.4.24   **Joseph Lingard**
Damare - The Wren

24.6.24   **Joseph Lingard**
Handel - Sonata No.1 in E

Debussy - Arabesque No.1

Boehm - Etude

23.12.24 **Joseph Lingard with Mavis Bennett (sop.)**

Bishop - Lo, here the gentle lark

2.1.25 **Joseph Lingard**

Kronke - Deuxieme Suite

Bishop - Lo, here the gentle lark (with Pat Ryan, clarinet)

Donjon - Offertoire

D. S. Wood - Valse-Caprice

Clinton - Valse Brillante (with Pat Ryan, clarinet)

19.3.25 **Joseph Lingard with Hallé Orchestra/Harty**

Godard - Suite

26.4.25 **Joseph Lingard with Charles Collier (harp)**

Mozart - Two movements from Flute & Harp

Concerto (w.piano)

Kronke - Suite in an ancient style (f1. & pf.)

Ilsa - Suite for flute & harp

21.5.25 **Joseph Lingard**

Revell - Trois Pensee

Widor - Romance & Scherzo

Bohm - Study

18.9.25 **Joseph Lingard**

Krantz - Suite

Hahn - Variations on a theme by Mozart

Bach - Sonata (BWV 1038) with Don Hyden (vln)

& Eric Fogg (pf)

1.11.25 **Manchester Wind Quintet (Joseph Lingard, flute etc.)**

Onslow - Quintet in D

Holbrooke - Miniature Characteristic Suite
Lefebvre - Suite in B flat
Pierne - Pastorale
Pessard - Prelude & Minuet
Barthe - Passacaille
Sobeck - Tarantelle
Taffanel - Quintet in G

29.11.25   **Joseph Lingard**
Handel - Sonata No.1 in E
Kohler - Oriental Serenade
Wood - Valse Caprice

4.2.26   **Willliam Thorn (in Lancashire Talent Series - Bury)**
Woodall - Serenade
Salonstuck - Fruhlingstimmen
Kronke - Gavotte & Courante (Suite in Ancient Style)
Le Thiere - Silver Birds (piccolo)
Filipovsky - Danse du Rissignol (piccolo)

7.2.26   **F. Whittaker with Lily Allen (sop)**
Bishop - Lo, here the gentle lark

4.4.26   **Manchester Wind Quintet (Joseph Lingard, flute etc.)**
Kouffmann - Quintet in E flat
Purcell - Cebell
Barthe - Passacaille
Sobeck - Scherzino
Val Hamm - Trio for flute, oboe & clarinet
Blumer - Dance Suite
Barthe - Aubade
Colomer - Minuet
Briccialdi - Allegro

5.5.26   **Joseph Lingard with Esther Coleman (voice),**
            Stephen Whittaker (ob) and Olga Thomas (pf)

Herbert Bedford - Night Piece No.2: The Shepherd

24.10.26   **Joseph Lingard (w.Eric Fogg, piano)**
Bach - Sonata in A
Handel - Sonata No.1 in E
German - Valse gracieuse
Godard - Allegretto
Mouquet - Pan et les Bergers

3.4.27   **Manchester Wind Quintet (Joseph Lingard, flute etc.)**
Rimsky-Korsakov - Quintet
Eric Fogg - Introduction & Allegro
Pierne - Pastorale
Colomer - Minuet
Barthe - Passacaille
Blumer - One Step
Sobeck - Tarantella

3.7.27   **Joseph Lingard**
German - Gracious Waltz, Souvenir, Gipsy Dance
Ingelbrecht - Esquisses Antiques
Paggi - Neopolitan Memories

26.7.27   **Joseph Lingard**
Kohler - Shepherd's Idyll
Debussy - Arabesque
Chopin - Waltz

21.8.27   **Joseph Lingard with J. F. Ridgway**
Loeillet - Sonata
Gaubert - Divertissement grec
Kronke - Suite, 'In the Olden Style'
Briccialdi - Brilliant Duet

16.10.27   **Manchester Wind Quintet (Joseph Lingard, flute etc.)**
Lefebvre - Suite

Blumer - Sarabande
Pessard - Prelude & Minuet
Holbrooke - Scherzo
Barthe - Aubade
Briccialdi - Finale from Quintet

20.11.27   **Manchester Wind Quintet (Joseph Lingard, flute etc.)**
Hoyer - Serenade in five movements
Blumer - Dance Suite
Pierne - Pastorale
Colomer - Minuet
Barthe - Passacaille
Sobeck - Tarantella

8.7.28   **Joseph Lingard with Augmented Station Orchestra**
Kohler - Shepherd's Idyll
Godard - Allegretto
Mouquet - Pan & the Shepherds
Blumer - Four Pieces

29.7.28   **Joseph Lingard with Otto Paersch (hn)**
& Station Orch/Morrison
Titl - Serenade (horn & orch)
Lefebvre - Idyll
Briccialdi - Carnival of Venice (flute solo)

17.3.29   **Joseph Lingard with Sir Hamilton Harty (piano)**
Harty - In Ireland

21.3.29   **Joseph Lingard with Hallé Orch/Harty**
Fuhrmeister - Gavotte & Tarantelle
(wind quintet & piano)

13.8.29   **Joseph Lingard**
York Bowen - Miniature Suite

10.11.29   **Northern Wind Quintet - Joseph Lingard (fl),**

Alec Whittaker (ob), Pat Ryan (cl),
Archie Camden (bn) & Otto Paersch (hn)
Lefebvre - Suite
Couperin arr.Setacioli - Trio for flute, clarinet & bassoon
Val Ham - Trio for flute, oboe & clarinet
(w. A. Camden, pf)
Barthe - Aubade
Colomer - Minuet
Grainger - Walking Tune
Sobeck - Scherzino
Pierne - Pastorale

8.5.30	**Joseph Lingard with Don Hyden (vln) & Eric Fogg (pf)** Bach - Sonata in C (Musical Offering) Mel-Bonis - Suite E.Goossens - Suite Op.6
26.9.30	**Joseph Lingard** (no programme details)
14.9.31	**Joseph Lingard with Muriel Liddle** (no programme details)
29.11.31	**Joseph Lingard with Eric Fogg (pf)** (no programme details)
5.1.32	**Joseph Lingard with Don Hyden (vln) & Eric Fogg (pf)** (programme details as 8.5.30)
22.3.32	**William Thorn** Kronke - Suite in the Ancient Style Brockett - The Mocking Bird (piccolo) Stainer - Valsette (flute) Green - Picaroon (piccolo)
12.6.32	**Joseph Lingard with Muriel Liddle (harp)** Paggi arr. de Jong - Rimemranze Napoletane Kronke - Caprice Impromptu

Hilse - Suite for flute & harp

17.6.32 **William Thorn**
Widor - Romance
Donjon - Rossignolet
German - Valse gracieuse; Gipsy Dance

12.5.33 **Joseph Lingard**
Andersen - Hungarian Fantasy
Maganini - Serenade
Dunhill - Waltz Fantasy

26.5.33 **William Thorn**
Briccialdi - Andante & Polonaise
D. S. Wood - Valse Caprice
Molique - Andante & Pollacca

25.2.34 **Hallé Woodwind Quartet - Joseph Lingard (fl),**
Fred Tilsley (ob), Harry Mortimer (cl),
Maurice Whittaker (bsn) & Eric Fogg (pf)
Fogg - Quintet

9.6.34 **William Thorn with Margaret Collier (sop)**
Getry - Recitative and Air
Benedict - The Gypsy and the Bird
Donizetti - Mad Scene (Lucia di Lammermoor)
Bishop - Mocking Bird Song
Bishop - Lo, here the gentle lark

6.9.34 **Joseph Lingard**
Handel - Sonata in F
Mouquet - Sonata - Pan's Flute
Soulage - Berceuse
Krantz - Tourbillon
Kronke - Caprice Impromptu

20.1.35	**Geoffrey Gilbert with BBC Northern Orch/Morrison**
	Mozart - Flute Concerto in D
19.4.35	**Geoffrey Gilbert**
	Mouquet - Pan et les Nymphes (La Flute de Pan)
19.6.35	**William Thorn**
	Godard - Allegro and Idylle
23.6.36	**Vernon Harris with BBC Northern/Procteer-Greg**
	Gluck - Scene on the Elysian Fields (Orpheus)
	(part of a complete performance)
26.7.36	**Joseph Lingard with Charles Collier (harp)**
	Hilse - Suite for flute & harp
5.11.36	**Joseph Lingard with Hallé Orch/H. Wood**
	Bach - Brandenburg Concerto No.5
16.4.37	**Joseph Lingard**
	Mouquet - Pan & the Shepherds
	Kronke - Caprice Impromptu
	Getry - Recitative & Air (Cephale et Procris)
	(with Margaret Collier, sop.)
	Paggi - Neapolitan Memories
	Bishop - Lo, here the gentle lark (with M. Collier, sop)
10.6.37	**Vernon Harris with BBC Northern Orch/Morrison**
	Mozart - Flute Concerto in D
27.10.37	**Joseph Lingard**
	Revell - Trois pensees
	Akimenko - Idylle
	Roussel - Tityre
3.1.38	**Norman Seville**
	Chaminade - Concertino
	Andersen - Waltz

30.4.39	**Vernon Harris with Charles Kelly (piano)**
	Cyril Scott - Scotch Pastoral
30.8.39	**Vernon Harris with BBC Northern Orch/Joseph Lewis**
	Bach - Suite in B
17.11.42	**Vernon Harris with Pat Ryan (cl)**
	& BBC Northern/Heward
	Saint-Saens - Tarantella
8.2.43	**Vernon Harris with BBC Northern Orch/**
	Julius Harrison
	Godard - Suite
29.1.47	**Vernon Harris with BBC Northern Orch/**
	Charles Groves
	Bach - Suite in B
29.12.50	**Oliver Bannister & William Barlow with**
	Hallé Orch/Markevitch
	Cimarosa - Concerto for Two Flutes & Orch.
1.3.51	**Oliver Bannister with BBC Northern Orch/**
	Charles Groves
	Frank Martin - Ballade for flute, strings & piano

NOTE: *Throughout the 1920's most, but not all, broadcasts from the Manchester station originated there. From the beginning of the 1930's the Manchester station was swallowed, with others, into the Northern Region station. During the War years all broadcasting* *throughout the country was of National or Forces programmes.*

APPENDIX 5

List of Compositions & Publications by Hallé Flautists

GILBERT, Geoffrey

| FLUTE METHODS: | Sequences | SMC, Texas 1990 |
| | Technical Flexibility | SMC, Texas, 1988 |

JONG, Edward de

| FLUTE METHOD: | National Flute Tutor (32pp) | Ascherberg, Hopwood & Crew Ltd., London |

FLUTE & PIANO:	A Little Story	Rudall Carte, London
	Ariel	Rudall Carte, London
	Bagatelle	Rudall Carte, London
	Caprice "Will o'the Wisp"	Rudall Carte, London
	Chanson sans parole	Rudall Carte, London
	Elegy	Rudall Carte, London
	Fantasia on Faust	Rudall Carte, London
	Fantasia on Scottish & Irish Airs	Rudall Carte, London
	Fantasia on Lucia Lammermoor	Rudall Carte, London
	Introduction et danse excentrique	Rudall Carte, London
	Moorland Fancy	Rudall Carte, London
	Norwegian Airs	Rudall Carte, London
	Polka de Concert	Rudall Carte, London
	Romanza	Rudall Carte, London
	Rondo Capriccioso	Rudall Carte, London
	Rondo a la Tarantelle	Rudall Carte, London
	Serenade	Rudall Carte, London
	Valse Caprice	Rudall Carte, London
	Valse du Printemps	Rudall Carte, London
	Valse Poétique	Rudall Carte, London

FLUTE, VOICE & PIANO: A Twilight Carol for soprano flute

| | and piano | Rudall Carte, London |

LAX, Fred

FLUTE METHOD:	Flute Method (287pp)	Pepper & Son, Philadelphia
FLUTE & PIANO:	Bonnie Scotland: Air & Vars.	Cundy Bettoney, Boston
	Fantasy on American Airs Op.88	Cundy Bettoney, Boston
	Fantasia on English Airs Op.86	Cundy Bettoney, Boston
	Fantasia on Irish Airs Op.78	Cundy Bettoney, Boston
	Fantasia on Mexican Airs (1887)	Alry Pub, Denver 1982
	Romanza	Cundy Bettoney, Boston
	Tarantelle	SMC, Texas
TWO FLUTES/PICCS & PIANO:	Twilight Carol Polka Op.112	Cundy Bettoney, Boston
PICCOLO:	Unique Polka	Hawkes & Son., London

PIDDOCK, W. H.

FLUTE & PIANO: Romance and Polonaise   Rudall Carte

Home Sweet Home   Rudall Carte

Bibliography

BATLEY, Thomas (ed)   Sir Charles Hallé's Concerts, in Manchester
Manchester, Charles Sever 1896

FUCHS, Carl   Musical & Other Recollections.
Sharratt & Hughes 1937

FITZGIBBON, H. Macaulay,   The Story of the Flute
William Reeves, London 1928

FLOYD, Angeleita   The Gilbert Legacy, Winzer Press, Iowa 1990

HALLÉ, C. E. (ed)   Life & Letters of Sir Charles Hallé
Smith Elder & Co., London 1896

HALLÉ MAGAZINE 1946-80   The Hallé Concerts Society/Hallé Club

HENSCHEL, Sir George   Musings & Memories of a Musician
Macmillan & Co., London 1918

KENNEDY, Michael   Barbirolli, Conductor Laureate
MacGibbon & Kee Ltd., London 1971

KENNEDY, Michael   The Hallé Tradition.
Manchester University Press, 1960

KENNEDY, Michael   The Hallé 1858-1983.
Manchester University Press, 1982

KENNEDY, Michael   The History of the Royal Manchester College of Music,
Manchester University Press, 1971

LORENZO, Leonardo   My Complete Story of the Flute, (Rev.ed)
Texas Tech University Press, USA 1992

REES, C. B.   100 Years of the Hallé, MacGibbon & Kee Ltd.,
London 1957

RIGBY, Charles   Sir Charles Hallé. The Dolphin Press, Manchester 1952

RUDALL, CARTE & CO. LTD   Photographs of Well-Known Flute Players,
Rudall Carte & Co. Ltd, London 1938